Traffic Tickets.

Don't get Mad. Get them DISMISSED.

Stories From The Streets

By Steven F. Miller and Alexis C. Vega

Revision: October 2012

Published by:

TicketBust.com
5716 Corsa Ave., Suite 104
Westlake Village, CA 91362

ISBN: 0615665624
ISBN-13: 978-0615665627

Prelude

No matter how careful you are it's going to happen to you.

No matter how closely you check the traffic lights and the cars in the other lanes, eventually it's going to happen to you.

No matter how aware you are of the road conditions and the other cars around you, it's still going to happen to you.

No matter how good and careful a driver you are, EVERYONE makes mistakes. And this mistake means that you're going to see those all too familiar red and blue lights in your rearview mirror.

The important thing is how you react to this situation. You could just pay the ticket and watch your bank account get hundreds of dollars lighter in ticket fees, court fees, and increased insurance premiums. Or you could try and fight it by taking time off from work, going down to court and dealing with court clerks, bailiffs, judges and the officer who issued the ticket. And you may still lose.

OR, you could do the smart thing. READ THIS BOOK. USE THIS BOOK. CALL TICKETBUST.COM.

Introduction

Last year we introduced you to our first book: *Traffic Tickets. Don't Get Mad. Get Them Dismissed. Traffic Ticket Tips, Must Knows, and Much More.* After this book was released we got to thinking about the over 50,000 cases that we have worked on and thought; "wow, we've heard some real stories and storytellers over the years." And then the idea hit us, "Let's share some of those stories." So we've put together several case studies that will walk you through the facts of the ticket and tell you about our solution that helped that driver "Get Off"; well, okay at least get their traffic ticket dismissed.

We've also put together many stories and excuses we've heard from drivers and why their traffic tickets did not get dismissed, these are the ones that "Didn't Get Off."

As good as these stories are we also wanted to give you some real hard-core information, tips and facts about traffic tickets, what works and what doesn't work, along with examining many traffic ticket myths in our truth or fiction section. We've also included all our information about what happens in traffic court and what to do if you do have to go to traffic court.

Now why should you care about what happened to another driver or how they got a traffic ticket dismissed or what lame excuse they had? Well that's easy; having the knowledge about what worked or didn't work for other drivers will make you better informed for when you get a traffic ticket. And you will, as the odds are not in your favor. The day will come when you see those flashing lights behind you or that quick flash of a camera as you realize that you just went through a red light with a red light camera device.

To give you an idea of what to expect, take the case of Jimmy; a few years ago Jimmy received a speeding ticket out in Barstow when his truck got a little away from him as he was going downhill. Jimmy tried to fight it on his own but couldn't get the ticket dismissed. Jimmy ended up with a point and a half on his driver's license and having to pay a pricey fine. There is a better way to contest a traffic ticket then going to court and trying it on your own. That's why you need to read this book and find out how other people had their traffic tickets dismissed.

Like Jimmy, before coming to TicketBust.com Angela tried to get out of a ticket, specifically a red light camera ticket, but no dice. Angela saw that flash go off and she knew she was going to get one of those red light camera tickets in the mail and she did. When she received it she knew that she wanted to fight the ticket so she waited for her court date to arrive and went to court. The officer at that court showed her a video of her clearly running right through that red light. Angela was lost and at that point just gave up and accepted her guilt. There is a better way!

If you are reading our book we're willing to bet you're like Jimmy, or Angela, and tried to get a traffic ticket dismissed on your own but didn't succeed. Or maybe you are just a first timer, not sure where to even begin. Whatever your reason may be, we are here to help and provide you some entertainment along the way. So sit down, relax, read our success stories, and the not so successful ones, and learn a thing or two about how you too can "Get Off" like the rest of them and get that traffic ticket dismissed.

About TicketBust.com

TicketBust.com has been around for over EIGHT years, helping drivers contest their traffic tickets and, in many cases, get those tickets dismissed. We have contested over 50,000 tickets in California and are sharing the information and knowledge acquired during that time with you. We don't believe that you need to just roll over and pay that traffic ticket. You have options and we are here to help you learn about those options.

Founded in 2004, TicketBust.com was originally created to alleviate the tedious and time-consuming process of attempting to contest a traffic ticket and to provide an online, user-friendly service for California drivers to submit their traffic ticket information and process the necessary documents. TicketBust.com, a Better Business Bureau Accredited Business with an A+ rating, assists drivers with fighting speeding tickets and other traffic tickets by using proven legal methods. One such method, Trial by Written Declaration, allows for a driver to contest a traffic ticket by mail instead of going into court.

In 2010, TicketBust.com released www.combatesuticket.com to assist the Spanish speaking community along with www.fightcellphonetickets.com to specifically address the needs of drivers receiving cell phone tickets. In 2011, to make it more convenient for drivers to immediately contest a traffic ticket, iTicketbust, a mobile application for iPhone and Android devices, was released. This is the only mobile application that will let you take a picture of your traffic ticket, input all your information and submit it to www.TicketBust.com to help you contest your traffic ticket.

Most recently, in 2012 TicketBust.com released an entirely new service to assist drivers contesting traffic tickets, www.tickethitman.com. TicketHitman.com is a fully automated system that can collect and gather all the required information needed to properly contest a California traffic ticket using a Trial by Written Declaration.

TicketBust.com released their first book entitled *Traffic Tickets. Don't Get Mad. Get Them Dismissed. Traffic Ticket Tips, Must Knows, and Much More* in 2011 and you are currently reading the follow up to that book. Like our first one, this book is a must have for anyone who has a traffic ticket, has ever had a traffic ticket, or may have a traffic ticket in the future.

You can also visit our web site at www.TicketBust.com for additional information. For Spanish speakers you may visit www.combatesuticket.com and for a cell phone ticket please visit www.fightcellphonetickets.com. You can even visit our latest service, www.TicketHitMan.com or download iTicketBust, our mobile application for iPhone and Android devices.

About The Authors

About Steven F. Miller Founder and president of TicketBust.com, Steve is the driving force behind the success and growth of TicketBust.com. Steve started TicketBust.com in 2004 with one goal in mind, to help drivers contest and dismiss their traffic tickets. Since then, Steve has continued to expand TicketBust.com by developing and deploying the necessary solutions to continue to assist drivers with contesting their traffic tickets. Steve has been a featured guest authority regarding contesting traffic tickets in California on many TV, Radio, and online networks.

In 2010 Steve released www.combatesuticket.com to assist the Spanish speaking community along with www.FightCellPhoneTickets.com to specifically address the needs of drivers receiving cell phone tickets and the fully automated www.TicketHitMan.com in 2012.

In 2011 Steve wanted to make it more convenient for drivers to immediately contest a traffic ticket so iTicketBust, a mobile application for iPhone and Android devices, was released. Steve's first book was released in 2011, *Traffic Tickets. Don't Get Mad. Get Them Dismissed. Traffic Ticket Tips, Must Knows, and Much More* and the follow up in 2012, *Traffic Tickets. Don't Get Mad. Get Them Dismissed. Stories From The Street. The Ones Who GOT OFF.*

Prior to TicketBust.com, Steve was CEO of MediaHippo, Inc., an interactive agency focused on web, DVD, and multimedia development. Steve graduated from California State University Northridge, with a BS in Accounting. Steve worked for Deloitte Haskins and Sells as a Certified Public Accountant, prior to starting his own accounting agency. Steve was instrumental in promoting and marketing the Kodak Photo CD technology in the

1990's, authored many articles and was a featured speaker at many industry events.

About Alexis C. Vega Coming from a family of law enforcement, her father being a retired California Highway Patrol Lieutenant, and other family members employed by the Glendale Police Department, Ventura Police Department, and the California Highway Patrol, Alexis has always had a special interest in the area of traffic tickets.

Alexis gained extensive experience while working as an intern at the Superior Court of California, Office of the Public Defender where she assisted with trial preparation and the California Court of Appeal researching and writing memorandum for the Appellate Justices. Alexis has also worked as an intern with the Law Offices of Ronald G. Harrington and Associates, assisting with *pro bono* case files. Alexis graduated from The Colleges of Law, Santa Barbara and Ventura, with the degree of Juris Doctor.

Alexis has helped to develop new strategies to help drivers get their traffic tickets dismissed; a continuing goal of hers. Alexis is now the Vice President, Legal Research & Case Analyst at TicketBust.com and uses her knowledge and experience to help train and mentor other TicketBust.com team members.

Alexis co-authored the 2011 release of *Traffic Tickets. Don't Get Mad. Get Them Dismissed. Traffic Ticket Tips, Must Knows, and Much More* and in 2012 co-authored *Traffic Tickets. Don't Get Mad. Get Them Dismissed. Stories From The Street. The Ones Who GOT OFF*. Alexis has also been a featured Radio Network Guest as an expert on all things to do with Traffic Tickets in the State of California.

Stories From The Street

Yeah, everyone has a story about the day they saw those flashing lights, heard that loud siren, and saw the police car in your rear view mirror. Holy Sh*t, you think to yourself, "There's no way I'm getting pulled over for a traffic ticket." "What the hell did I do?" "There's no way he saw me do that? He couldn't have!!!"

Then you settle down and think to yourself "How am I going to get out of this?" Maybe you could tell the officer the gas pedal stuck? But then realize he's probably heard that before. So you wonder what other story would he believe? Maybe you could try a few of these:

Put on some dark sunglasses and get a long stick and pretend you are blind and couldn't possibly have been driving.
See http://www.youtube.com/watch?v=KZ-iqT3Q_wg&NR=1

If you're a handyman, use some electrical tape and hop in the passenger seat, tape yourself all up and pretend you've been kidnapped.
See http://www.youtube.com/watch?v=5_7SWvNAvWY

Maybe you've got a bunch of plants in your car? Grab them and place them in front of the window and hide. Maybe the officer won't see you.
See http://www.youtube.com/watch?NR=1&v=rtSlc5YM5mQ

If you're driving with an animal, like a dog, trade places with the dog and pretend the dog was driving.
See http://www.youtube.com/watch
v=M4jCiAtPQxo&feature=related

Let's say you just went through your favorite drive-through and had a few left over ketchup packages. Rip them open, squirt them

all over you and pretend you're dead.
See http://www.youtube.com/watch?v=MgY-7uvNvXY

This one only works for some. Take a bottle of water and as the officer is approaching, pour it down the front of your shirt and see if he lets you off.
See http://www.youtube.com/watch?v=8Rvb58HZQ2k&feature=related

Although most of the stories above won't really get you out of a traffic ticket, they would make great coffee-table talk.

You Just Got Pulled Over, What Now?

Getting pulled over for a traffic ticket can be a traumatic experience. What do you do when you get pulled over? What should you say to the officer? More importantly, what should you not say when getting pulled over? Based on discussions with clients and our years of experience, TicketBust.com has put together a list of things to do and things to avoid doing.

We provide these tips to all our clients. In fact, we have produced a handy "Glove Box Folder" that includes all our traffic ticket tips printed right on the folder. Keep this folder in your car as an easy reminder and also place a copy of your insurance and registration inside the folder. You can refer to this folder any time you get pulled over by an officer.

Anyone that signs up for our service at www.TicketBust.com receives our "Glove Box Folder" mailed to them automatically. We have also provided you a list of our 50 Traffic Ticket Tips below:

Tips for when you are pulled over by an officer

1. Stay Calm

2. Pull over safely and quickly to the right

3. Signal when pulling over

4. Pull far enough over so the officer can stand without getting hit

5. Remain in your vehicle, unless the officer instructs you to get out

6. Ask for identification if the officer is not uniformed or you're uncertain

7. Roll the driver's side window all the way down

8. Turn off your engine

9. Lock your doors

10. Place the car keys on the dash

11. If it's dark out, make the officer more comfortable by turning on the dome light

12. Keep both hands on the steering wheel

13. Leave your seatbelt on

14. Be courteous - this may result in a reduced penalty or warning

15. Ask permission before reaching for items

16. Tell the officer what you are reaching for and where it is

17. Follow the officer's instructions

18. Remember you have the right to remain silent

19. Keep a car wallet with insurance, registration & copy of license

20. Keep pad and pen in car - for writing down details of the stop

21. Keep a camera in the car - go back as soon as possible to take pictures of the area where you were stopped

22. If you work or live close to the County Seat and would prefer to have your case moved there, you have the right to request it

23. Keep all your answers brief and non-incriminating

24. When leaving, pull out safely and use your signal

25. If you have passengers in the car, ask them to remain silent unless spoken to first by the officer

26. If the officer asks: "Do you know why I pulled you over?" The safest answer you can give is: "No, I was driving safely"

What NOT to do when you get pulled over by an officer

1. DON'T admit guilt to any particular speed (or anything for that matter)

2. The officer is not required to show you his speed gun, DON'T argue if he answers no, instead, make a note for use later

3. DON'T take pictures, do or say anything memorable in front of the officer

4. DON'T linger and write down notes for more than a second or two after a traffic stop

5. DON'T let the officer know you plan to fight the ticket

6. DON'T make any sudden movements

7. DON'T offer any info. Always wait for the officer to ask

8. If the officer says "no" to your request to have your ticket transferred to the County Seat? DON'T argue, just write "county seat requested" next to your signature

Tips for when you are caught on camera

1. Go back and time the yellow light with a stopwatch

2. Check if any camera enforcement warning signs were posted and where they were posted

3. Note if you made any turns or went straight (same is true for a stop sign or non camera red light)

Tips for when you get a speeding ticket

1. If you're pulled over for speeding, take note of how fast the officer said you were going

2. If the officer asks "How fast were you going?" The ONLY good answer is: "A safe and reasonable speed"

3. Make note of the location, road conditions, traffic, and weather

4. Keep track of any and all statements that the officer makes; but take no more than a few seconds to jot them down when officer goes back to his car

5. Make note if there were or are any pedestrians, schools, or parks nearby

6. Note where the officer was when you first saw him

7. If the officer is carrying a radar or lidar speed gun and the officer shows it to you, don't make any comments about it, but do try to note the manufacturer and model of the device

8. If the officer did not use a radar/lidar device, note how long the officer was following you

Tips for when you get a stop sign ticket or red light ticket

1. Note where in relation to the limit line both you and the officer were when the light turned red

2. Take pictures from the officer's view and note any obstructions of both the limit line and the stop sign

3. If asked why you didn't stop for a stop sign a safe answer is: "I didn't proceed until safe"

4. If there is a posted sign, take pictures of the sign and anything blocking it - note anything that could have prevented you from seeing it

What to do after you get a ticket

1. Remember that TicketBust.com is on your side!

2. Go to our web site at www.TicketBust.com and select the "To Bust My Ticket Now" option or "Start Right Now." Just fill out the information and we will do the rest

3. Remember if you have a mobile phone you can download our iTicketBust App and take a picture of your ticket and submit it via your mobile device. Go to http://www.ticketbust.com/app-page.html

Let's Review The Traffic Ticket Fighting Process

So you've decided to fight that traffic ticket. Well good for you. After having spent nearly a decade successfully fighting for our clients, we're here to tell you it's very possible to win. You just need to know what you're doing.

The eight steps below explain how we go about fighting those tickets. It may seem complicated, but when you've prepared and filed over 50,000 Trial by Written Declaration documents, you get a pretty good idea of how to do it effectively and successfully. That's one reason our clients keep coming back. They like to win. So let's get started:

Step 1. Determine what type of ticket you received

We first need to ensure you were cited for a type of ticket that TicketBust.com can help you contest. We determine this by identifying the type of ticket you were cited for, which court your ticket is filed with, and when your ticket is due. Once we have identified the type of ticket you have involves a non-parking, moving violation (i.e. red light, stop sign, speeding, cell phone tickets), that is filed with a Superior Court of California (tickets filed with the U.S. District Federal Court cannot be contested in writing using California's Trial by Written Declaration method), that is current and not past due (tickets that are past due or have gone to collections are no longer eligible to be contested using the Trial by Written Declaration), we get to work narrowing down exactly what law the officer states you violated.

Step 2. Research Violation Code listed on ticket

We review your traffic ticket and identify the violation code. This is not always easy for the layman to identify. Most do not know what the term violation code refers to. Even more aren't aware of where to look. The violation code on most tickets is found smack dab in the middle of the ticket (below all your personal information like your name, address, vehicle information, and insurance company). The violation code is usually accompanied by a subsection and possibly a subdivision and it is equally important to obtain this information to ensure you are referring to the correct law. However identifying the correct violation code is not always cut and dry as some may have lost the ticket or cannot read the officer's writing. TicketBust.com's expert ticket consultants are well trained in deciphering an officer's markings on a ticket and, if the violation code is not available, can even determine most violation codes by simply looking at the facts of your case. As an example, an unknown violation code for a speeding ticket can be determined by factoring in the speed limit, the cited speed, the type of vehicle being driven at the time, the class of driver's license you have, the number of lanes on the highway you were driving on, and the location (whether the violation occurred on a city street or a freeway).

Step 3. Identify whether the violation is a traffic infraction or a misdemeanor

In researching the violation code we must also determine whether you have been cited for a traffic infraction or a misdemeanor. Most are not aware of the difference or what either means. It is important to identify which one you were cited for so that you know your rights under the law and what potential penalties you might face if convicted. A traffic infraction is a less serious offense (like speeding, red light, stop sign, cell phone tickets). You need to know that for a traffic infraction you are allowed a traffic trial, either in person before a judge with your accuser (the officer) present or a trial in writing (Trial by Written Declaration) and that if you are found guilty after a Trial by Written Declaration you are allowed a new trial (*trial de novo*) in person before a judge with your accuser (the officer) present. The penalties for a traffic infraction include fines but not jail time. A misdemeanor on the other hand is a more serious offense (driving while unlicensed, drunk driving, driving a grossly overweight truck, driving a commercial truck at 15 mph or more above the legal limit) and you could face jail time in addition to a fine. Since you could potentially face jail time, in some instances you are allowed a trial by jury and to choose to have a court appointed public defender to help you if you can't afford your own lawyer. You can look to the same area where the violation code is found and following the violation code there should be an 'I' or a 'M' circled. This tells you if you were cited for an infraction or misdemeanor and only traffic infractions can be fought using a Trial by Written Declaration.

Step 4. Search for any exceptions to the law

Once we have identified the violation code for the traffic infraction for which you were cited, we can get to work researching that law using our library of electronic and paper references that we have compiled over the years. There are often exceptions to each law that can be applied to an individual case. For example, the law states you cannot drive over double yellow lines. However this is not an absolute law. There are exceptions like if you are turning into or out of a driveway, turning left at an intersection, or making a U-turn. We always check for exceptions to the law because many times we find that officers tend to overlook these exceptions and issue a ticket when one was not justified in the first place.

Step 5. Contact client for facts surrounding incident

After we have taken the time to thoroughly research a particular violation, we take the opportunity to contact you to review the facts of your case. Each violation is different and depending on the violation you were cited for there are certain details that will be more relevant than others. Plus judges have a limited amount of time to spend reviewing your case and do not have the time or patience to thumb through pages of irrelevant details in order to get to the meat of the issue. TicketBust.com has expert traffic consultants who are trained on how to weed through insignificant details to get the real important facts that help get tickets dismissed. All relevant details are carefully documented to be used later and combined with our own independent research in preparing a proper statement for dismissal.

Step 6. Apply facts to exceptions to law to determine if any are applicable

We take the facts you have provided based on your best recollection of the day you received the ticket and compare the facts to any exceptions laid out in the law you were cited for. Any exceptions that are applicable are noted in order to be later used and combined with other possible defenses.

Step 7. Research possible defenses & review past cases that have been dismissed for use of similar defense

Having the ability to review past traffic cases that have been dismissed gives us better knowledge as to what defenses tend to be successful with the court. We also determine if there are any other defenses that can be applied based on the facts of your case, such as if there was an emergency situation or other mitigating circumstance. In every case we work to create doubt in the eyes of the court that the officer actually saw you breaking the law and work to create doubt as to whether the officer's determination was accurate. For example if you provide details that, at the time you committed the infraction or misdemeanor for which you were cited, it was dark and the officer was preoccupied issuing a ticket to another motorist we can create enough reasonable doubt to show the officer could not have correctly identified your speed.

Step 8. Prepare a Trial by Written Declaration statement using all applicable defenses

This is the final step in fighting your ticket. Based on our independent research of the violation for which you were cited, together with the facts gathered by us from you, and using all defenses and exceptions to the law that we have found are applicable to your case, we prepare a solid request for dismissal. It is then documented onto Trial by Written Declaration forms and all documentation, together with any supporting evidence such as photographs or witness statements you have provided, are submitted by TicketBust.com to the court on your behalf.

So, there you have it. There are a lot of little details and know-how involved, but when you've filed as many Trial by Declaration document packages as we have, you'll find that they're all important; you develop a good sense of what to say, what not to say and what works. So, are you ready to put all that experience to work fighting your ticket?

Step 1. Determine what type of ticket you received

Step 2. Research Violation Code listed on ticket

Step 3. Identify whether the violation is a traffic infraction or a misdemeanor

Step 4. Search for any exceptions to the law

Step 5. Contact client for facts surrounding incident

Step 6. Apply facts to exceptions to law to determine if any are applicable

Step 7. Research possible defenses & review past cases that have been dismissed for use of similar defense

Step 8. Prepare Trial by Written Declaration statement using all applicable defenses

Traffic Ticket Terminology

General traffic court terminology and traffic terms broken down into plain English.

Acquitted The court has declared that you are innocent.

Appearance Date This is the date listed on your ticket or courtesy notice. You must take some sort of action by this date whether it is submitting a Trial by Written Declaration, making an appearance in court or paying the cost of the ticket, it has to be done no later than this date.

Appeal If you are dissatisfied with the decision a judge made after a court trial you are sometimes able to file an appeal to try and have that judge's decision overturned. Appeals are often complex and complicated and most people have an attorney assist them with it, although you can contact the court for the necessary paperwork and filing deadlines.

Arraignment This is just a court appearance where you can tell the court how you intend to plead (i.e. guilty/not guilty). This isn't an actual trial where the officer is present. If you want a court trial or Trial by Written Declaration you can request one at this time and you'll be given a new date to appear for the trial.

Bail This is the cost of the ticket as determined by the court. If you plan on fighting the ticket, it's referred to as bail because you can potentially be refunded the money you paid the court if your ticket is dismissed.

Bailiff maintains overall courtroom order, security and custody of the jury. In Traffic Court, this is the officer who will take any documents needed from you and provide them to the Judge.

Calendar The cases set for hearing or trial in a specific department, on a given date and time, are referred to collectively as that department's calendar.

Calendared The specific date, time and department for which a case has been set, whether for hearing or trial, is said to have been calendared.

CHP The California Highway Patrol.

Clocked This term is generally used to describe when an officer gets or determines or observes your speed using whatever method it may be (i.e.: radar, laser, visual, air plane).

Citation Another name for a traffic ticket.

Contest This is a term used to refer to "fighting a ticket."

Correctable Violation This means you can obtain proof of correction and pay a small fee to get rid of the ticket. No traffic school is necessary for a correctable violation.

Courtesy Notice This is the notice sent to you by the court, generally several weeks after you receive the ticket from the officer. The courtesy notice will tell you your options for fighting the ticket, tell you how much the ticket will cost you, and tells you the date by when you must handle the ticket. If you don't receive a courtesy notice you must still contact or appear in court no later than the date listed on your ticket, a courtesy notice is just that, a "courtesy," it's not a mandatory notice that the court MUST send to you.

Dismissal Order or judgment finally disposing of an action, motion, etc.

Entering a Plea When you make a plea to the court you are essentially telling the court whether you did it (guilty), didn't do it (not guilty), or I do not want to say whether or not I did it (no contest).

Failure to Appear This means you didn't take care of your ticket by the deadline. The court can add an additional fee to your original ticket fine or bail and continued failure to comply can result in your case being referred to a collections company, suspension of your driver's license, or a warrant for your arrest.

Infraction This is a term used to describe a minor offense such as a speeding ticket. You can generally only be fined for committing an infraction as compared to being punished by a fine and or jail time for a more serious offense like a misdemeanor.

Laser / Lidar Another type of electronic speed measurement device which is used to pinpoint and pick up the speed of a specific vehicle to which the officer has a clear line of sight. Laser and lidar are used interchangeably, however all California Highway Patrol tickets uses the term lidar whereas a ticket issued by a local city police officer will almost always use the term laser.

Misdemeanor This is a term used to describe a more serious offense such as driving without a license.

MVR Motor Vehicle Record. You can obtain an unofficial copy of your driving record on the CA DMV website for a small fee. http://www.dmv.ca.gov/online/onlinesvcs.htm http://www.dmv.ca.gov/online/onlinesvcs.htm

Notice to Appear This is the official term used to describe a ticket or citation.

Pace A method used by law enforcement whereby the officer follows another car to estimate the speed.

PD The Police Department.

Points Points are "demerits" that show up on your California driving record and can cause your license to be revoked or suspended depending on the number of points you have in a given period of time. If you are found guilty of your traffic ticket, traffic infraction or traffic violation, after you pay your fine, additional points may show up on your DMV record unless you can go to traffic school. If the court lets you go to traffic school and you turn in your proof of completion of traffic school to the court before the deadline, the points should not show up on your record. If you get points on your record, for any reason, your insurance company may ask you to pay more for insurance, or they may cancel your policy and tell you to find insurance elsewhere. Points can stay on your record for 3 to 7 years.

Radar A type of electronic speed measurement device which is used to pick up on the speed of the fastest moving target in range. Radar can be used in the stationary or moving mode.

Traffic school If you are found guilty of your traffic ticket, after you pay your fine, points may show up on your DMV record unless you go to traffic school. If the court lets you go to traffic school and you turn in your proof of completion of traffic school to the court before the deadline, the points should not show up on your record. The court can tell you what you need to do to be able to go to traffic school. If this is your first ticket and the court lets you go to traffic school, you should not get any points on your record. In addition to the court fees, the traffic school will also charge you for the class. It will take a whole day to complete. Some courts let you go to traffic school on the web. As long as you have not been to traffic school in the last 18 months and the court honors traffic school for the type of violation you committed, you will get traffic school upon requesting it from the judge. According to Vehicle Code section 42005 and pertaining to *People v. Wozniak*, you can still have the option to attend traffic school even after you have been found guilty of the alleged violation.

Trial This is when you exercise your right to request an in person court trial with the officer present so you can present your case in front of a judge.

Trial by Declaration (Form TR-205) A way you can fight or contest your ticket in writing without going into court.

Trial De Novo (Form TR-220) If you fight your ticket using a Trial by Declaration and are found guilty then you have the right to request a new trial within 20 days. *Trial de novo* means a "new trial" and if a *trial de novo* is granted to you it is treated as if no prior trial had been held.

Violation Code This is the number written on the ticket and which usually appears on the courtesy notice as well, and this number represents the offense committed. Generally the letters V and C will appear before the number and these letters don't represent Violation Code, rather they are used to indicate "Vehicle Code" Example: VC 22349 (a). This means you were cited for subsection 'a' of section 22349 of the vehicle code and if you were to look up that section you would see that it appears under Speeding over the maximum of 65 mph.

Visual A method used by an officer whereby the officer who is trained to make visual estimations, essentially "eye balls" your speed.

We Got Them Off, We Can Get You Off Too!

Everyone loves a good success story and boy do we have some good ones for you. These drivers came to us feeling down on their luck, with circumstances that were unique to them but commonplace for us and as you must have guessed by now...we got them off without a problem. Leaving them with no fines, no points, and no worries!

So let's get this started. All the cases below, presented along with the facts and the solution(s) we provided that helped get their traffic ticket dismissed, are based on 100% real traffic ticket cases (however, we have changed the names to protect the innocent). We know this because they all come from our extensive list of case files. In fact you may feel like some of these cases actually happened to you and think to yourself "what would I do in this situation"? Well we'll tell you what our clients did and what we did to Get Them Off.

Case Study #1–Urinating On Freeway

Circumstances

This one's from the "there's no way this is true" department, but believe me this case study along with all the others contained in this book are 100% real traffic ticket stories.

We've all found ourselves in this same situation. You need to go to the bathroom while you're driving but there's just nowhere to go. So what do you do? Most of you would hold it, no matter how much it hurt, until you found a rest stop, gas station, restaurant or some other facility that has a bathroom. A few of you would just pull over on the side of the road and relieve yourself right there because, hey, who's going to stop you?

So here's the situation. Mr. Smith from Anaheim was driving back from Las Vegas after playing in a Basketball Tournament. He had been drinking lots of fluids on the way because he was dehydrated from playing in the Tournament. Obviously the more fluids you drink the sooner you're going to need to relieve yourself.

Dehydration often happens without athletes realizing it and much fluid is lost through sweating. Players need to drink plenty of water before, during and AFTER a game as they will lose quite a bit of water during game play. Being dehydrated can lead to early fatigue and since he was driving home at 2:00 am, he did not want to fall asleep at the wheel.

Mr. Smith was driving in a deserted area on the I-15 North bound where there were no exits anywhere nearby, no people, and no cars on the road. The area was completely empty. He pulled off on the side of the road and crawled down in a ditch so that he could relieve himself of his urgent need to urinate. As he was re-entering the car the officer drove up behind him.

Before he knew it, Mr. Smith was cited for violation 23112(a), which states "No person shall throw or deposit, nor shall the registered owner or the driver, if such owner is not then present in the vehicle, aid or abet in the throwing or depositing upon any highway any bottle, can, garbage, glass, nail, offal, paper, wire, any substance likely to injure or damage traffic using the highway, or any noisome, nauseous, or offensive matter of any kind."

Yes, ladies and gentleman, urinating on the side of the road does qualify as "depositing...offensive matter" onto the highway.

Solution
Violation 23112(a) does require a mandatory appearance in court. Since Mr. Smith did not did not want to make the court appearance he called TicketBust.com to help him contest and get his traffic ticket dismissed.

First thing we did was send a letter to the court requesting them to waive the mandatory appearance and set bail. The court obliged, and bail was set at $481.00. We then proceeded to complete and file his Trial by Written Declaration with the court.

In our research we found that CVC §21462 applied to emergency type situations, providing an exemption from the law for certain persons faced with an emergency: "The driver of any vehicle, the person in charge of any animal, any pedestrian, and the motorman of any streetcar shall obey the instructions of any official traffic signal applicable to him and placed as provided by law, unless otherwise directed by a police or traffic officer or when it is necessary for the purpose of avoiding a collision or in case of other emergency, subject to the exemptions granted by Section 21055."

As such, we believed that a similar rule could be applied here. This was similar to an emergency situation since Mr. Smith's actions were out of necessity, and not out of any ignorance of the law. There were no exits nearby and no prospect of a truck stop or restroom facility anywhere nearby. He was essentially left with no other alternative.

Conclusion

Here's what happened. We submitted the Trial by Written Declaration on Mr. Smith's behalf. The court reviewed the declaration and also reviewed the police officers response to the declaration and issued its decision.

In this matter the court found Mr. Smith Not Guilty of this violation and returned his bail in the amount of $481.00 in full. The ticket was dismissed!!!

No, we don't suggest that if you need to relieve yourself that you just pull over and do it where ever you please, but if the facts and circumstances are aligned with the one's in this case you may just have a chance of getting out of this type of traffic ticket if you were ever to receive one.

As a footnote, we are told that Mr. Smith does use a restroom whenever possible but now does travel with a portable potty just in case the urge to urinate ever does arise again.

Case Study #2–Collecting Recyclables On Freeway

Circumstances

This one's from the "no good deed goes unpunished" department...

In this "Go Green - Eat Organic - Buy Hybrid" day and age, the last thing you'd expect is to get a ticket WHILE in the act of doing the good deed of recycling.

So here's the situation: Ms. Thompson from Wrightwood, CA was driving on the freeway through San Bernardino County. While traveling, she happened to observe some mixed recyclables off on the shoulder. The thought of ridding the road of this debris and recycling for the good of the earth (and putting a few extra dollars in her pocket, too) was just too tempting to resist.

Ms. Thompson was driving in very heavy traffic, which had actually come to a complete stand-still. She figured she could pull to the side of the road, grab the cans and bottles, and be back in her car before traffic even started moving again.

She was physically picking up the recyclables when the officer approached her and was shocked to hear she was receiving a ticket for a "Non-Emergency Stop."

Specifically Ms. Thompson was cited for 21718(a), which says "No person shall stop, park, or leave standing any vehicle upon a freeway..." (with some exceptions).

Officer "Non-Eco-Friendly" did not feel picking up recyclables fit into any exception.

Solution

Ms. Thompson did feel her actions were justified and felt the ticket resulted from the good act of recycling-an act that should be commended, not criminalized. So she came to TicketBust.com for help in resolving this ticket.

First thing we did was work on finding how we could apply the act of recycling into one of the several exceptions laid out in the law under which Ms. Thompson was cited.

In our research we found that CVC §21718 says there are these exceptions to the law:

- When necessary to avoid injury or damage to persons or property.

- When required by law or in obedience to a peace officer or official traffic control device.

- When any person is actually engaged in maintenance or construction on freeway property or any employee of a public agency is actually engaged in the performance of official duties.

- When any vehicle is so disabled that it is impossible to avoid temporarily stopping and another vehicle has been summoned to render assistance to the disabled vehicle or driver of the disabled vehicle. This paragraph applies when the vehicle summoned to render assistance is a vehicle owned by the donor of free emergency assistance that has been summoned by display upon or within a disabled vehicle of a placard or sign given to the driver of the disabled vehicle by the donor for the specific purpose of summoning assistance, other than towing service, from the donor.

- Where stopping, standing, or parking is specifically permitted. However, buses may not stop on freeways unless sidewalks are provided with shoulders of sufficient width to permit stopping without interfering with the normal movement of traffic and without the possibility of crossing over fast lanes to reach the bus stop.

- Where necessary for any person to report a traffic accident or other situation or incident to a peace officer or any person specified in paragraph (3), either directly or by means of an emergency telephone or similar device.

- When necessary for the purpose of rapid removal of impediments to traffic by the owner or operator of a tow truck operating under an agreement with the Department of the California Highway Patrol.

We found that an exception DID apply to the facts of Ms. Thomson's case. You see, she was in effect, acting in accordance with the first exception which allows for a non-emergency stop "when necessary to avoid injury or damage to persons or property." The debris on the pavement posed a potential traffic hazard since it is completely likely that a tire could be punctured by glass or other recyclable debris depending on the type and condition of the tire!

We were able to convince the court that the mixed recyclables on the pavement including glass bottles, posed a traffic hazard because a tire could potentially be punctured if the wind caused the glass to roll into traffic or if someone, in the act of pulling to the side to avoid an accident, had driven across it. So she had good cause to stop and pick up the recyclable debris.

Conclusion
In response to the Trial by Written Declaration that we prepared and sent to court for Ms. Thompson, she received a not guilty verdict and a refund of her $240.00!

Thankful to have had it dismissed, but bitter from getting ticketed in first place, the former Ms. "Eco-Friendly" Thompson has since traded her Prius for a Hummer, stopped buying groceries from Whole Foods, and no longer sorts her garbage for aluminum cans.

Case Study #3–Long Haul Trucker Receives a "Long Haul" of Multiple Traffic Tickets

Circumstances

Obviously if you drive for a living the chances of getting a ticket will increase. It's a fact, drive more, and you'll receive more tickets. There's just no way around it. It's also a fact that when you drive for a living, your livelihood depends on it. You can't afford to have tickets on your driving record for fear of losing your job. It's imperative that you keep your driving record clean. You can usually live with one ticket but multiple tickets are a sure death sentence.

So here's the story, Mr. Hill, is a commercial driver based out of Sparks, Nevada. He depends upon a good driving record to keep his job during these difficult financial times. He came to TicketBust.com in late 2009 with a speeding ticket (VC-22406) and then a few months later he received an over weight ticket (VC-35551). A speeding ticket and a weight violation could have put Mr. Hill's license, and therefore his job, in jeopardy.

Solution

Violation Code Section 35551 Computation of Allowable Gross Weight states the following:

> 35551. (a) Except as otherwise provided in this section or Section 35551.5, the total gross weight in pounds imposed on the highway by any group of two or more consecutive axles shall not exceed that given for the respective distance in the following; Distance in feet between the extremes of any group of 2 or more consecutive axles.

The vehicle code goes on to show the maximum total gross weight in pounds imposed on the highway by any group of two or more consecutive axles for the distance in feet between the extremes of any group of 2 or more consecutive axles.

In this case, Mr. Hill was stopped at the truck scales in the Cajon Pass while traveling northbound on the I-15 in San Bernardino.

The total weight of the truck was 77,940 pounds however the weight on his rear axles was not properly distributed and was over by 1,000 pounds (Axle 1 = 11,400 pounds, Axle 2/3= 31,020 pounds, and Axle 4/5 35,520 pounds). It turns out that the improper weight distribution was unknown to Mr. Hill at the time and upon being pulled over, he immediately corrected the problem by pulling the load over to one spot.

Even though Mr. Hill corrected the weight distribution upon the issue becoming known to him, the officer still issued him a ticket.

Mr. Hill's, second ticket was related to California Violation Code Section 22406, Maximum Speed for Designated Vehicles, which states the following:

> 22406 (a). No person may drive any of the following vehicles on a highway at a speed in excess of 55 miles per hour:
>
>> (a) A motor truck or truck tractor having three or more axles or any motor truck or truck tractor drawing any other vehicle.
>>
>> (b) A passenger vehicle or bus drawing any other vehicle.
>>
>> (c) A school bus transporting any school pupil.
>>
>> (d) A farm labor vehicle when transporting passengers.
>>
>> (e) A vehicle transporting explosives.
>>
>> (f) A trailer bus, as defined in Section 636.

In this case we identified that Mr. Hill was just entering a downhill stretch of road with his truck, carrying a heavy load. We indicated that he began to brake, however he felt that he could not place too much pressure on his brakes for fear the brakes would heat up and fail due to the heavy load he had in his truck, creating a danger to himself and others. Additionally, there was also another 18-wheeler in front of him and he was concerned that if his brakes did fail he would slam into the truck in front of him.

Conclusion

Both of Mr. Hill's tickets were dismissed and NO points were posted on his driving record as a result of both dismissals. Mr. Hill's total bail of $577 was also returned to him in full, within 60 days of the court finding him not guilty on each count.

Mr. Hill knew that if those tickets ended up on his permanent driving record that his job would be in jeopardy. He just could not take that chance. He knew he needed a professional to make sure that both his tickets were contested properly.

In the case of the over weight ticket, since we were able to demonstrate that in total his truck was within the allowable limits and that he was not aware that items had shifted so that the back axle was over weight and that he immediately corrected it upon discovery, the court found him not guilty and dismissed the ticket.

The speeding ticket was also dismissed as we were able to prove that there was a potential danger to other people and vehicles if Mr. Hill did in fact apply too much pressure to his brakes while traversing the downhill portion of the road.

Two things should be noted from Mr. Hill's cases:

If you are unaware that something is wrong or incorrect with the vehicle you are driving and the officer brings it to your attention, you should immediately correct it, if possible, as this shows your willingness to comply with the law.

Sometimes the necessity to ensure that public safety is not jeopardized can supersede actual traffic law, as we found in Mr. Hill's speeding case.

Case Study #4–The Joplin Tornado

Circumstances
Ever found yourself in a situation where you knew you were breaking the law but had a compelling reason to do so? Mrs. Hunt did.

Mrs. Hunt was overcome with worry while driving on a quiet afternoon in Riverside County. Her stepson was in Joplin, Missouri at the time when a Tornado struck. This Tornado was said to be the deadliest since 1950 and was ranked 9th among the deadliest Tornados in United States history.

She received a phone call from an out of state area code while driving and quickly answered it, as she had been on pins and needles waiting to hear if her stepson was ok. This resulted in her receiving a ticket for California Vehicle Code 23123 (hands free device required to talk on a phone while driving) and she came to TicketBust.com for help.

Although she technically had broken the law, she felt it was undeserved given the circumstances, and felt any judge who had children could understand as they probably would have done the same thing in her shoes.

Solution
After reviewing the facts of her case our team of case consultants decided the best way to persuade the court to dismiss this ticket would be to emphasize the gravity of the situation with the Tornado and to quote past court decisions relating to cases where courts had decided a traffic law wouldn't necessarily be considered an absolute rule under all circumstances (such as emergency situations).

We were able to demonstrate that Mrs. Hunt's actions in utilizing her phone to talk to her stepson during a time when she had reason to believe he was in danger due to a natural disaster, were out of necessity given the severity of the situation, not out of ignorance of the law.

Conclusion

Mrs. Hunt was pleased to have her stepson return home, unharmed; and was equally pleased to receive the court's notice of "not guilty" and a refund of the $210.00 bail she had posted with the courts.

Case Study #5–Beyond A Reasonable Doubt

Circumstances

Ms. Roberts, from Pleasant Hill, CA, is a very responsible 56-year-old woman and a prudent driver. Her line of work requires her to have a spotless driving record. Like all of us, she wants it to remain that way.

Unfortunately her perfect driving record was put in jeopardy on a rainy, winter day in 2009 when Ms. Roberts found herself being tailgated by another driver. As she frequently drives the busy Bay area freeways, she has a tactic that she uses for regular tailgaters she finds behind her.

Normally she would just tap her brakes two or three times to warn the driver behind her to back off, and usually they do. On this particular rainy, winter day, when she was presented with a tailgater and wanted to use this tactic, she couldn't because the roads were wet so she felt it was not safe to do this.

As Ms. Roberts says, "My only choice was to get out of the way and to let the larger vehicle pass by me. If the road was dry I would not have had to switch lanes I could have just tapped my brakes and the other driver might have backed off. However, today I had to change lanes and increase my speed to allow the other driver to pass."

As a result, she was pulled over. As Ms. Roberts described the instance, "On the day I was issued the citation, I was driving westbound on the I-580 Freeway amongst moderate traffic. The roadway was multiple lanes wide and free from construction or debris. Overall, I was driving at a speed which was reasonable or prudent having due regard for weather, visibility, the traffic and the surface and width of the roadway."

Solution

Ms. Roberts was cited for CVC 22349(a) California Speeding Violation - According to the DMV this violation is described follows:

Maximum Speed Limit 22349:

(a) Except as provided in Section 22356, no person may drive a vehicle upon a highway at a speed greater than 65 miles per hour.

(b) Notwithstanding any other provision of law, no person may drive a vehicle upon a two-lane, undivided highway at a speed greater than 55 miles per hour unless that highway, or portion thereof, has been posted for a higher speed by the Department of Transportation or appropriate local agency upon the basis of an engineering and traffic survey. For purposes of this subdivision, the following apply:

> (1) A two-lane, undivided highway is a highway with not more than one through lane of travel in each direction.

> (2) Passing lanes may not be considered when determining the number of through lanes.

(c) It is the intent of the Legislature that there be reasonable signing on affected two-lane, undivided highways described in subdivision (b) in continuing the 55 miles-per-hour speed limit, including placing signs at county boundaries to the extent possible, and at other appropriate locations.

Ms. Roberts found hope when she discovered TicketBust.com. Since the officer was not relying on the use of radar or lidar, a TicketBust.com Traffic Ticket Expert explained exactly what we would need from Ms. Roberts in order to prepare and file her Trial by Written Declaration.

Ms. Roberts was informed that in order to contest her traffic ticket using a Trial by Written Declaration, she would first have to post bail and, once the traffic ticket was dismissed, the court would refund her bail.

Unlike some services, TicketBust.com uses the court's Trial By Written Declaration documents to contest traffic tickets. Some services simply give you a downloadable eBook which describes a traffic ticket defense, and then leaves the paperwork filing and everything else up to the driver. At TicketBust.com we submit all documents to the court on behalf of our clients, so the client doesn't have to go to court or even the post office.

TicketBust.com had a conference call with Ms. Roberts and helped her formulate the defense that TicketBust.com then used in her Trial By Written Declaration defense documentation as follows:

> "The officer alleged that I was traveling at 82 mph and I did not admit any guilt as to traveling at that speed. I felt my speed was reasonable and prudent in light of the circumstances (driving conditions and traffic). The officer cited me for allegedly violating VC§22349 by traveling at 82 mph in a 65 mph zone, however the officer did not rely on the use of radar, and I believe the officer was mistaken in citing me for that speed.

> "I had to switch lanes more than once because I was being tailgated. I actually accelerated as a result of seeing a car closing in behind me (and the roads were slick because it had been raining earlier so I feared being rear ended), feeling it was impossible for me to both adhere to the Maximum Speed Law, yet also adhere to the Basic Speed Law, when it was safer for me to speed up due to the car pushing me from behind, and my presumption was that they wanted to get past me. I ended up changing lanes and the officer was behind me. However the officer was not behind me long and did not use radar to assess my speed. The foregoing reasons would explain why he cited me for a speed in excess of my actual traveling speed.

"It must be proven beyond a reasonable doubt that I was traveling at the cited speed and thus guilty of this infraction. However, the officer seemed to be relying only upon his own speedometer for his visual speed estimation. A subjective visual estimation of speed is the least credible type of method an officer may use to assess a vehicle's speed. In my case, only his actual training records containing information regarding the accuracy of his visual estimations of speed, with the use of a calibrated speedometer, might be cited as evidence to possibly prove beyond a reasonable doubt that his visual speed measurement in this instance was credible, and if he has produced no such records, then he is incompetent to rely solely on his own visual estimation of my speed without the use of radar or lidar instrumentation. Perhaps to enhance his speed estimate's credibility, the officer may have used a comparative measurement, for example if I was catching up to or passing another vehicle. However, in my particular case, I was not gaining on, or attempting to overtake, any other vehicle. I do not feel I was traveling at the speed I was cited for, and since the officer did not rely upon the use of any calibrated radar or laser instrumentation for speed measurements, I feel he mistakenly came to the conclusion that I was traveling at 82 miles per hour.

"The lack of evidence of any speedometer calibration is also relevant to this inquiry. If the officer testified that his car was going 82 mph while he was following from behind me, he has the burden to prove beyond a reasonable doubt that his speedometer reading was based upon a calibrated reading. Otherwise, even if he stated that his speedometer read 82 mph while following my vehicle, this reading itself may have been an incorrect indicator of my vehicle's true speed. As with instrumentation such as radar or laser/lidar, the patrol car's speedometer should have been calibrated by a certified shop before and after the officer's shift. It is highly unlikely that such a timely speedometer calibration was performed. In California, it is required to test any speed measuring device within a reasonable time, such as those in highway patrol cars. Only if the officer presented evidence that calibration was performed upon the officer's specific patrol car used that day can we even begin to reasonably consider that the speedometer measurement itself could have been correct at the time of citation issuance. Thus, for example, if the officer states that he followed behind my vehicle at 65 mph, this statement alone, without reliable proof, constitutes impermissible hearsay. Proof of a calibrated speedometer in the officer's specific vehicle that was calibrated to accurately measure speed at the time of the citation is lacking in this case."

Conclusion

In March of 2010, Ms. Roberts wrote to us, "I posted a 5-star review at the Better Business Bureau, and gave your web site address to everyone I know to bookmark it in case they ever need help. One of my friends probably already contacted your company. I don't know how to thank you for all your help, for the very smooth processing, and for the result!"

Then she added the following, posted on TrustLink.org, she wrote "At the end of last year I got pulled over for speeding 82 mph in a 65 mph zone on a rainy day. I had no experience in how to try to explain to the Officer why I did what I did, just handed over the documents he asked for. I did not want to go to court either because I am not good at talking publicly, so I searched the internet and found TicketBust.com. The web site explains everything very clearly, and I signed up for help. I sent all documentation (very few) back they sent me to sign with my check for the bail amount, and in a few days a representative called me for some details. From that point all I had to do is wait."

Upon receiving a notice that the case had been dismissed and she would be getting a full refund of her bail amount, Ms. Roberts had these comments which she gladly posted on the internet, "A month after the court date I received a letter from the court dismissing the case and indicating that my full bail amount would be returned in 60 days! Everything went very smoothly, and everyone who contacted me either on the phone or by email was very nice and professional. I already gave their web site address to my friends if they should ever need help. Thank you TicketBust.com!!!!"

Case Study #6–The Natural Disaster

Circumstances

"I was married once–in San Francisco. I haven't seen her for many years. The great earthquake and fire in 1906 destroyed the marriage certificate. There's no legal proof. Which proves that earthquakes aren't all bad."
–W.C. Fields (American Comic and Actor, 1880-1946)

The same (earthquakes aren't all bad) can't be said for Ms. Logan who got a speeding ticket while trying to outrun one.

Here's the story:

Ms. Logan and her kids were visiting California from out of state. One night, while on their vacation, they encountered a truck hauling a trailer with animals that overturned while trying to avoid rocks falling onto the freeway.

They next encountered Border Patrol agents who were directing traffic. When they stopped to ask the officers what had happened, the Border Patrol Officer blurted out: "It's an earthquake. You're not safe here. Get out of here!"

Being from out of state and never having experienced an earthquake, they took this Border Patrol Officer at his word and sped up to put distance between them and the area which was unsafe as a result of the earthquake.

Just minutes later they were pulled over by a CHP officer and cited for speeding.

Solution

Feeling strongly about fighting the ticket, Ms. Logan enlisted the help of TicketBust.com, who found out that:

The California Vehicle Code section that Ms. Logan was cited with, 22356 (b), did not give any direction as to what would happen if there was a natural disaster, it only stated, "No person shall drive a vehicle upon that highway at a speed greater than 70 miles per hour, as posted."

TicketBust.com traffic ticket consultants got to work searching for cases that dealt with some sort of emergency situation. They did in fact find a case they felt was relevant. The driver had technically broken a law but due to emergency circumstances the court found their conduct justified and found them exempt from the law. TicketBust.com consultants beefed up the request for dismissal by including articles that local papers had published the day after the incident outlining the intensity of the earthquake. This illustrated for the courts the severity of the situation.

Conclusion
The officer didn't buy the story about trying to outrun the earthquake, but with Ticketbust's help, Ms. Hunt was able to prove to the court that a ticket was unjustified in this instance given the circumstances and did not even have to waste time appearing in court to correct the injustice.

Case Study #7–The Grinch Couldn't Ruin This Christmas

Circumstances

"And the Grinch, with his Grinch-feet ice cold in the snow, stood puzzling and puzzling, how could it be so? It came without ribbons. It came without tags. It came without packages, boxes or bags. And he puzzled and puzzled 'till his puzzler was sore. Then the Grinch thought of something he hadn't before. What if Christmas, he thought, doesn't come from a store. What if Christmas, perhaps, means a little bit more."
–Dr. Seuss

On the day Ms. Keys from San Ramon, California was issued a citation, the winter holiday season was in full swing. In fact, it was the heavy shopping season just prior to the holidays. Ms. Keys was looking forward to the holidays which she would spend with her seven grandchildren and nine nephews. She was driving northbound on the US-101 Freeway amongst moderate traffic about five hours away from her home.

Although it had been raining earlier, the weather was mostly clear. Overall, Ms. Keys was being prudent, having due regard for weather, visibility, the traffic and the surface and width of the roadway and was driving at a speed which was reasonable for the conditions.

She was traveling with a group of cars when she observed the patrol car in her rearview mirror. As Ms. Keys states, "I did not know at first that I was getting pulled over and I presumed the officer wanted to get by me to go after another car."

Unfortunately, the officer was not pulling over another car; rather Ms. Keys was the vehicle the officer was after. The officer turned on the lights in the patrol car and Ms. Keys was directed to pull over. Of course she immediately developed that sinking feeling in her gut as many of us do.

Naturally when you get pulled over for a traffic violation you begin to run various scenarios through your mind as did Ms. Keys.

"Was I going too fast?"

"Did I use my blinker properly when changing lanes?"

"Did I pull over with a safe distance from the traffic lanes?"

"Do I have the proper paperwork handy like my insurance card and registration?"

"Should I reach for these documents now or wait until the officer asks for them?"

"Should I turn the car off?"

"Should I get out of the car, roll down my window, or wait for instructions from the officer?"

Solution
The officer cited Ms. Keys for traveling at 83 mph; however she did not admit any guilt as to traveling at that speed. She felt her speed was reasonable and prudent in light of the circumstances (driving conditions and traffic). The officer cited Ms. Keys for allegedly violating VC§22349 (a) by traveling at 83 mph in a 65 mph zone.

According to the DMV this violation's description follows:

Maximum Speed Limit—22349 (a):

(a) Except as provided in Section 22356, no person may drive a vehicle upon a highway at a speed greater than 65 miles per hour.

(b) Notwithstanding any other provision of law, no person may drive a vehicle upon a two-lane, undivided highway at a speed greater than 55 miles per hour unless that highway, or portion thereof, has been posted for a higher speed by the Department of Transportation or appropriate local agency upon the basis of an engineering and traffic survey. For purposes of this subdivision, the following apply:

> (1) A two-lane, undivided highway is a highway with not more than one through lane of travel in each direction.

> (2)Passing lanes may not be considered when determining the number of through lanes.

(c) It is the intent of the Legislature that there be reasonable signing on affected two-lane, undivided highways described in subdivision (b) in continuing the 55 miles-per-hour speed limit, including placing signs at county boundaries to the extent possible, and at other appropriate locations.

Ms. Keys was a keen driver and went to the Internet for help. She found TicketBust.com, a professional document filing company that helps California drivers dismiss or reduce their speeding, and other traffic tickets. The experts at TicketBust.com helped her put together a Trial by Written Declaration and submitted all the necessary documents to the court for her.

This declaration, included details such as:

> "The officer could not have had a clear line of sight to her car amongst all of the nearby vehicles that were traveling the same speed as Ms. Key's car or faster," and she believed the officer was mistaken in citing her for that speed.

> "I do not feel the officer was behind me for long and I believe that the patrol car quickly gained on me from behind. I noticed the officer quickly closed the gap between my car and his patrol car (having the effect of giving him an artificially high speedometer reading), and if he was not constantly examining his speedometer (which is likely he did not because he would have been focused on his own

driving and his speedometer all the while ensuring other motorists were driving safely and following his target vehicle), then he would have glanced down at his speedometer as he was closing in on me and used the accelerated speed as a basis for the ticket.

"I am not aware that the officer followed behind me for any defined distance (for example the officer made no indication on the ticket that he followed me from point A to point B) while traveling the same speed and not faster than me. The foregoing reasons would explain why he cited me for a speed in excess of my actual traveling speed."

Some of the other arguments we helped her discover included:

The lack of evidence of any speedometer calibration is also relevant to this inquiry. It appears that in addition to a visual speed observation with use of a speedometer, the officer may also have relied upon a radar device.

For radar to be as accurate as possible, there are some conditions that must be met, including a flat and straight road, good visibility, and a minimum of traffic, and the officer has to be properly trained to interpret false signals generated by the equipment. The radar unit should be calibrated before and after each violation with the tuner fork supplied by the manufacturer.

By the time Ms. Keys' Trial by Declaration documents were finished, there was much more information included, and previous cases cited, when the final declaration was submitted to the court by TicketBust.com.

The declaration concluded with the statement, "As one final seemingly insignificant note, the officer wrote my zip code incorrectly on the citation. This minute detail may seem insignificant on its face however it does raise the possibility that the officer may not have been paying close attention to detail and raises doubt as to whether he clocked and cited me for the accurate speed at which I was traveling at."

Conclusion
The fine for this ticket was $414.00 and being the holiday season, it was especially difficult for Ms. Keys to afford. However in order for Ms. Keys to fight her traffic ticket using the California Trial by Written Declaration, she was required to post this fine with the court prior to, or at the same time, that she submitted her Declaration.

This was a problem that Ms. Keys discussed at length with her case consultant at TicketBust.com. It was decided that we would submit her California Trial by Written Declaration with a letter requesting the court to waive bail and proceed with the Declaration. Even though it is the law that you submit your bail with the Declaration, the court waived this requirement and allowed Ms. Keys to proceed with her Trial by Written Declaration.

We submitted her Trial by Written Declaration to the court on December 10, 2009. On February 11, 2010, Ms. Keys received her decision notice from the court: NOT GUILTY. The court found reasonable doubt that she did what the officer alleged that she did.

Ms. Keys wrote TicketBust.com a wonderful note about her experience with us: "Thank you Ticket Busters. I got my speeding ticket in a town five hours from home. My ticket was for $414.00 due just after Christmas. Because of your help, I didn't have to make the trip to court. My seven grandchildren and nine nephews never knew that Christmas was potentially in jeopardy and best of all my insurance company is none the wiser. I would recommend you to anyone with any kind of traffic ticket."

Case Study #8–Every Parents' Worst Nightmare

Circumstances

Ms. Knight, barely twenty years old had just found out...every parents' worst nightmare...she was pregnant.

Feeling scared, and alone, and knowing her dad was going to hit the roof, Ms. Knight immediately thought to call her confidant, her sister. Only one problem, she was driving at the time she made the phone call.

An officer of the Glendale Police Department happened to be patrolling Glendale Boulevard and he spotted Ms. Knight driving, phone in hand.

Ms. Knight was immediately red-lighted and directed to pull over.

To make matters worse, just moments prior, she had spilled a drink and had to remove her seatbelt in order to retrieve it from the floorboards.

Ms. Knight got cited for not only a cell phone violation but also a seatbelt violation. What's more, she couldn't find her license at the time so she got cited for that as well. Could it be any worse?

Solution

Ms. Knight was concerned about the ticket showing up on her driving record mostly because she was still on her parents insurance and if their rates increased because of her they would flip. This, combined with having to break the news that she was pregnant, was too stressful for her.

She turned to TicketBust.com for help.

TicketBust.com consultants prepared a written declaration on Ms. Knight's behalf based on inside research and knowledge combined with the facts Ms. Knight provided asking the court to consider among other things, that per California Vehicle Code section 21462: "The driver of any vehicle, the person in charge of any animal, any pedestrian, and the motorman of any streetcar shall obey the instructions of any official traffic signal applicable to him and placed as provided by law, unless otherwise directed by a police or traffic officer or when it is necessary for the purpose of avoiding a collision or in case of other emergency..."

Though dealing with a seatbelt provision and not a traffic signal provision per se, the court could apply a similar rule in this case since Ms. Knight's reason for removing her seatbelt was to avoid having the spilled drink roll underneath her brake pedal causing her pedal to become stuck in the upright position where an accident could have easily resulted if Ms. Knight lost control of the vehicle and couldn't stop.

As for the cell phone use while driving, TicketBust.com consultants felt the court would be more lenient given the extreme situation and fact Ms. Knight was not a repeat offender when it came to cell phone use while driving. It was her first cell phone ticket ever and her declaration pointed to the fact that she had actually just been dialing at the time the officer pulled her over so the phone was not actually in use and the law governing cell phone use while driving does not specifically prohibit dialing.

Conclusion
Ms. Knight may have had to deal with breaking the news of her pregnancy to her parents but she was thankful to TicketBust.com for not having to divulge the existence of the ticket.

Ms. Knight's bail amounted to over $340.00 and had she just paid it outright, the ticket would have been recorded on her driving record and her parent's insurance premium would undoubtedly have gone up.

Case Study #9–One Client's Day In Court

Circumstances

The beauty of a Trial by Written Declaration is that it doesn't eliminate your right to have your day in court or your right to traffic school. Even though a Trial by Written Declaration is an excellent way to contest a traffic ticket, not every ticket is dismissed using a Trial by Written Declaration and small percentage of our clients do not get their tickets dismissed with our service. In these cases, we ask our clients to call us as soon as they get their results from the court, as the court will allow you to have a new trial (known as a *trial de novo*), but a written request must be received by the court within 20 calendar days of the court's decision. If notified by our clients, we will process the necessary documents for a new trial on our client's behalf.

The *trial de novo* (or "all things new" in Latin) is always in your best interest, as it is your second chance to try to get your traffic ticket dismissed. Here at TicketBust.com we are strictly a professional filing agency, not a law firm so we do not offer representation for our clients in court and our clients make the court appearance on their own. However, we do provide them with all the information from their original Trial by Written Declaration to use in court so they are confident when they make their appearance.

For example, our client, Mr. Little from Bermuda Dunes, CA unfortunately had this occur with his ticket. We filed the Trial by Written Declaration and after the court took it under consideration he was still found guilty. Every judge is different so fighting your ticket twice and having your case reviewed by a different judge often results in a different judgement. Therefore, when Mr. Little let us know the results of his case, we advised him to file a *trial de novo*, form TR220. After we processed the *trial de novo*, the court approved the request and Mr. Little received a notice of the trial date and time in March 2010.

Solution

The beauty of a *trial de novo* case is that all facts are new as this is a new trial and not an appeal. This is your second chance to contest your traffic ticket with a fresh start. The court does not take into consideration anything that was said in the original Trial By Written Declaration so you can present totally different facts or use the same set of facts used in the original Trial By Written Declaration documents. It's entirely your choice.

In Mr. Little's case, there were only three cases on the court calendar that day. He observed those three cases, and all three officers showed up. However, we have found that officers are less likely to show up on a *trial de novo* than they would on an original court date. This is true because the court date is extended so far out, in many cases up to a year after the original ticket was issued, that it is less likely that the officer attends the court trial.

Mr. Little immediately noticed that his judge appeared to be at least 10 years younger than he was. The judge had a Norwegian name. The officer that had issued his ticket showed up for this court date. Both the officer and Mr. Little wore a suit, with a tie, the officer was very clean-cut, with no tattoos or earrings and was a nice guy, but very young.

Luckily Mr. Little 's case was not the first cased called that day and he was able to observe the case that was tried prior to his. We always recommend that you pay careful attention to how the judge reacts to defendants in cases tried prior to yours as a way for you to gather some valuable insights in how your judge thinks and reacts.

The first offender poorly presented his case. This offender was cited for hitchhiking on the freeway next to his truck because his big rig broke down. He even presented evidence of his truck being towed, but still lost the case. Technically he was hitchhiking and Mr. Little thought that maybe he was "in big trouble with a tough judge" as he put it. The third offender left due to the officer showing up in court.

When Mr. Little's case was called, both the officer and Mr. Little were sworn in. The judge asked the officer to present his case. The officer read his entire written testimony from his original Trial By Written Declaration, which Mr. Little had picked up a couple of days prior to his hearing. With *trial de novo* cases, we recommend that you request a copy of the officer's written declaration because it gives you the advantage of knowing beforehand what the arguments will be against you in court. This can help you decide how to present your case at your new trial.

According to Mr. Little, when the officer finished presenting his case, the judge asked him, "Do you have any other evidence?" The officer said no.

Conclusion

To Mr. Little's surprise, he won his case and his ticket was dismissed. As he states, "Amazingly I won due to sheer luck and a technicality. The judge said the officer failed to identify me in court when he presented his case against me."

Here is what happened. After the officer presented his case, the judge asked Mr. Little if he had any questions for the officer. Mr. Little replied that he did not have any questions for the officer and that he would like to move on to making his statement. The Judge said, "You don't have to make a statement you can choose to remain silent. Do you still want to make a statement?" Mr. Little said "Yes."

The Judge then said to Mr. Little, "Are you sure? I [the judge] said you can choose to remain silent?" Mr. Little replied "Yes" again while looking directly at the Judge and the Judge shook his head from side-to-side a little, as if to give Mr. Little a heads-up to remain silent. So Mr. Little said, "No, I would like to remain silent."

The Judge immediately said to the courtroom, "CASE DISMISSED due to the officer not identifying the subject [Mr. Little] in presenting his case."

As Mr. Little was conveying his story to us, he concluded, "The officer and I talked as we walked out and riding the elevator together. The officer and I were very friendly, he said, 'Boy that worked out well for you.' I told him I was hoping he wouldn't show, but he said they pay him too well not to have shown up. I told him my case was basically the way I stated it in my written declaration. He told me they are not allowed to see the written declarations. I think this is a big advantage for the driver. I then asked him how often they have to have their speedometers calibrated and he said every three months. I told him in my case with him, it had been five months." This was the argument Mr. Little was going to make.

We believe that Mr. Little's ticket would have been dismissed after he presented the facts if he had that opportunity. However his ticket was thrown out on a technicality. Oh well, does it really matter why a ticket is dismissed as long as it is dismissed? Mr. Little was extremely happy with the results even though he did not have a chance to present his case to the court.

Case Study #10–Least Likely to Succeed

Circumstances

If you are going to drive over the speed limit on a busy street, make an unsafe lane change, fail to yield to an emergency vehicle, while driving a car with an illegal modified exhaust pipe, at least don't do it in front of a police station!

Mrs. James did all the above, and yes it was right in front of a police station where a cop happened to be pulling out of the driveway for the start of a shift.

Thinking she had a loser case, but desperate to avoid a $1,000.00 plus fine and multiple points that could cause the DMV to suspend her license, Mrs. James came to TicketBust.com looking for answers and hoping for the best.

Solution

Despite committing the multiple violations all at once and in front of the officer, working with the details and facts Mrs. James provided, TicketBust.com was able to construct a rational and convincing defense for Mrs. James to use in fighting her ticket.

As far as the alleged unsafe lane change and speed, it was proven that Mrs. James was forced to speed up and change lanes to avoid an accident when an SUV stopped short directly ahead of her and failed to signal for a right hand turn.

As for failing to yield to the emergency vehicle, this vehicle was actually the citing officer's patrol car, and it was proven that Mrs. James pulled into the first available safe location and that it was not feasible to stop any sooner because the only other place she could have stopped was an abandoned lot that she felt would have been unsafe on account of her being a lone female with two small children in the car.

As for the modified exhaust pipe, she had not been aware at the time of the incident that the exhaust pipe was illegal and proof was shown to court that the exhaust pipe was removed and replaced with a street legal one.

Conclusion
It took a couple months to hear back from the court but it was worth the wait for Mrs. James who had been biting her nails thinking she wouldn't prevail. The court decision came back dismissing every single charge. She received a refund in the full bail amount of over $1,000.00, and even better, she avoided having three points added to her record (one more point and she would have been dubbed a negligent driver by the DMV and could have had her license suspended).

Case Study #11–Two Time Winner, Twice As Much As Most People

Circumstances

Mr. Birch, from Los Angeles California is a two time TicketBust.com client who had previously had a case for speeding on the Bay Bridge completely dismissed as a result of using the TicketBust.com service, and hoped that if it worked the first time it would work again.

Since it had been about a year and a half since his last ticket, Mr. Birch decided it was time to go speeding again and get another ticket. This time the ticket was for going 80 mph in a 65 mph zone in Solvang, California. As such, Mr. Birch found himself 'in the hot seat' again.

On the day of the alleged violation, Mr. Birch was driving south bound on the 101 freeway at approximately 5:00 pm. There was a moderate amount of traffic on the roadway and the weather was clear. Mr. Birch was going with the flow of traffic and was within a pack of about ten cars traveling with him. The officer was positioned on the side of the road and did not have a clear view of Mr. Birch's car due to amount of cars surrounding him. As it so happens, modern cars tend to look alike and Mr. Birch believed that the officer had mistakenly targeted his vehicle instead of one of the other one's traveling next to him.

Although Mr. Birch was traveling at a safe speed and with the flow of traffic, he was pulled over and cited for Maximum Speed Limit violation 22349(VC).

According to DMV this violation description follows:

> (a) Except as provided in Section 22356, no person may drive a vehicle upon a highway at a speed greater than 65 miles per hour.

> (b) Notwithstanding any other provision of law, no person may drive a vehicle upon a two-lane, undivided highway at

a speed greater than 55 miles per hour unless that highway, or portion thereof, has been posted for a higher speed by the Department of Transportation or appropriate local agency upon the basis of an engineering and traffic survey. For purposes of this subdivision, the following apply:

> (1) A two-lane, undivided highway is a highway with not more than one through lane of travel in each direction.

> (2) Passing lanes may not be considered when determining the number of through lanes.

(c) It is the intent of the Legislature that there be reasonable signing on affected two-lane, undivided highways described in subdivision (b) in continuing the 55 miles-per-hour speed limit, including placing signs at county boundaries to the extent possible, and at other appropriate locations.

Solution

Mr. Birch had used the TicketBust.com document filing service for a previous traffic ticket and told us that he remembered how professional and competent the TicketBust.com staff was. He also remembered that his first traffic ticket was DISMISSED and his bail refunded with no demerit points added to his driving record. Mr. Birch knew that if he didn't use TicketBust.com's help on this new, alleged speeding ticket, he would be out the bail amount and could expect a significant increase to his automobile insurance premiums.

He contacted the TicketBust staff and a traffic ticket expert discussed the circumstances of the Violation Code - 22349. Once this discussion about the circumstances was complete, TicketBust.com formulated a Trial by Written Declaration on Mr. Birch's behalf in an effort to get the ticket dismissed from the court. Here's an excerpt of the defense put forth on Mr. Birch's Trial by Written Declaration:

> "I was going with the flow of traffic and was within a pack of about ten cars. The officer was positioned on the side of the road and did not have a clear view of my car due to amount of cars surrounding me. Also, modern cars tend to look alike and I believe the officer mistakenly targeted my vehicle. Traveling at a safe speed with the flow of traffic, I was pulled over and cited for violation 22349 (VC). I would like to inform the court, the alleged speed the officer has indicated on my citation is incorrect. It is evident the officer has relied upon a radar unit to assess the speed I was driving. I would like to inform the court; the officer appeared behind me and signaled to pull over. At no point did the officer have a clear line of sight on my car to determine the speed I was driving."

Additionally, in California, in order to contest a traffic ticket, the court requires you to post bail for a Trial by Written Declaration (If you post bail directly with the court, you must inform the court that you are posting bail for a Trial by Written Declaration to contest your ticket. The court will refund your bail if your ticket is dismissed). Therefore, Mr. Birch had to also include a bail check, made out to the court.

The Trial by Written Declaration is the critical document for defense and for Mr. Birch's ticket certain points were argued, complete with previous case citing, regulations on the proper use and maintenance of radar guns, officer's line of sight, number of vehicles sharing the roadway and more.

Conclusion
Mr. Birch is now batting 1,000 with two for two tickets dismissed using TicketBust.com's service. The Trial by Written Declaration was filed and all Mr. Birch had to do was wait (30 to 90 days) to hear back from the court. Before he knew it, the court notified him

directly as to the disposition of his case, DISMISSED! Was all he needed to hear.

After receiving yet another favorable notification from the courts, Mr. Birch wrote to TicketBust.com to express his gratitude as follows, "I have worked twice with this company to get traffic tickets dismissed. They do traffic tickets, not parking tickets. Both times, the ticket was completely dismissed and my money refunded by the court. I don't know how they do it, but it works. They charge about $250 total for all the fees and depending on your situation, it may or may not be worth it. For me, I used them to fight an expensive ticket, and a cheaper ticket. In both cases, it worked and no demerit points were added to my record. So even for cheap tickets, you may want to consider using them to fight a ticket just so your record isn't tarnished by demerit points, which will lead to increases in your insurance premiums. I definitely recommend them, they seemed very courteous and honest when I talked to them (honestly, by that I mean they listen to your story and write a case for dismissal based on it and they don't distort anything), and never had a problem dealing with them. More importantly, it works."

Case Study #12–Case of Mistaken Identity

Circumstances

In 2011, the City of San Bernardino (following a decision coming from a San Bernardino court ruling that tickets issued from red light cameras were hearsay and thus not admissible) tried to shut down its cameras and stop issuing red light camera tickets by June 1, 2011

Unfortunately for Mr. Gaines his wife didn't make it through a stop light in time before it turned red at an intersection in San Bernardino, the cameras flashed as she went through, and a week or two later they received a ticket with her picture on it dated June 1, 2011 in the mail.

Mr. Gaines was in quite the predicament. He wasn't the one driving the vehicle but he got the ticket because he was the registered owner of his and his wife's car. The back of the ticket listed options to handle the ticket. One option was to fill out an affidavit stating it was someone else driving and to name that person. This option was out for Mr. Gaines because his wife recently got a ticket on her way back from Vegas for failing to come to a complete stop at a stop sign. Too many points on her record would put her driving privilege at risk and also bring costly increases to their insurance premium.

The back of the ticket also gave instructions on how to pay the fine and to close out the case. Mr. Gaines didn't feel this was the right option either. It didn't seem fair given the fact San Bernardino had said they were supposed to be closing down their cameras the same day his wife got the ticket. The thought actually crossed his mind that he should just rip up the ticket and throw it away since it could possibly be invalid.

He also saw options for fighting the ticket through a court trial but he didn't know what he would say to the judge since he wasn't the driver and he didn't want to tattle on his wife. Unsure of how to best handle the situation Mr. Gaines enlisted the help of TicketBust.com.

Solution
TicketBust.com had to help Mr. Gaines prepare his case quickly because he called with only four weeks left until his case was due in court. His case had to be prepared carefully because Mr. Gaines didn't want anyone to find out it was his wife driving at the time of the ticket. He also didn't want to say outright that he wasn't the driver for fear the court may ask him to disclose the identity of the driver.

The solution was to cite recent local court decisions ruling that tickets issued from the cameras were hearsay and not admissible, as well as news articles reporting that the City of San Bernardino wanted its red light camera program shut down on June 1, 2011, the very day Mr. Gaines' ticket was issued.

It was further argued that on top of everything else, the Police Department had issued a ticket to Mr. Gaines based on photographic evidence gathered from a red light camera of a driver of a vehicle that had absolutely no resemblance to Mr. Gaines. And that it was the Police Department's duty as the issuing governmental agency to identify the driver prior to issuing the citation and as it was shown by providing a copy of Mr. Gaines ' driver's license... he looked nothing like the driver pictured on the ticket.

Conclusion
Although the City of San Bernardino was ultimately unsuccessful in being able to shut down their cameras as they had announced they would (due to an existing contract that could not be broken without penalty), Mr. Gaines and his wife WERE successful. The court refunded the outrageous $490.00 fine that Mr. Gaines had to pay to the court when he posted bail for the ticket and more importantly the ticket was dismissed with no questions asked. He never had to disclose anything about his wife being the driver at the time of the ticket, and no points went on his driving record.

Case Study #13–Red Light Tickets Could Cost Almost $2,000

"Everyone wants to live at the expense of the state. They forget that the state wants to live at the expense of everyone."
–Frederic Bastiat (statesman, philosopher, author, leader, economist, and witty satirist, 1801-1850)

Circumstances
Local and state governments need money to run and one of the largest revenue generators for local and state governments are traffic tickets. Without the money that the government generates from traffic tickets there would be serious cuts in many social programs.

Mrs. Sandro received a red light traffic ticket and called us up crying. She couldn't afford the cost of the ticket, not to mention how it would affect her insurance. We calmed her down so that she could talk. She just couldn't believe how they could get away with charging so much for this ticket. She told us if her husband found out, he would "kill her" (he would actually just be very mad, but even so we do not promote or condone violence).

Mrs. Sandro's actions on the day she was issued the citation for allegedly committing an infraction of the California Vehicle Code Section 21453 included:

- Approaching a traffic controlled intersection at Lost Hills and Las Virgenes, in Calabasas, CA;

- There was moderate traffic that day and the weather was gray;

- She came to the limit line as the light was changing to yellow and since the light was not yet red when she came to the limit line, she was not required to stop.

This didn't matter as the police officer that pulled Mrs. Sandro over issued her a ticket for a red light infraction while making a right-hand turn on what she perceived to be a yellow light. The California Vehicle Code Section 21453 Circular Red states:

> 21453. (a) A driver facing a steady circular red signal alone shall stop at a marked limit line, but if none, before entering the crosswalk on the near side of the intersection or, if none, then before entering the intersection, and shall remain stopped until an indication to proceed is shown, except as provided in subdivision (b).

Mrs. Sandro's ticket cost close to $500, and her estimated total increase in insurance over a 3-year period was about another $1,200; serious money!

Solution
When contesting a red light traffic ticket, or most tickets for that matter, there are several factors that should be addressed in your statement. They include but are not limited to the following:

- Burden of proof is upon the people;

- Pursuant to Cal. Penal Code §1096, the people must prove their case beyond a reasonable doubt;

- Should the officer fail to respond to the Trial by Written Declaration with a declaration of his own, the people will have failed to prove their case, and a dismissal of the citation is appropriate due to lack of prosecution;

- Any mitigating factors for the court to consider when determining whether a dismissal is warranted;

- Conditions or factors which may have prevented the officer from having a clear line of sight to the vehicle on the day of the issuance of the citation;

- In order for the officer to have been in a position to gather substantial evidence for use in judging guilt or innocence, the officer needed to have a clear line of sight to the vehicle, the traffic signal itself, and the limit line for the traffic signal.

Here is an excerpt from this client's Trial By Written Declaration:

"I would like to address VC§21452 which states in part that a yellow light means only that traffic facing the light is warned that a red light will soon follow. It is not illegal to deliberately drive through a yellow light. So long as my vehicle entered the intersection, or passed the crosswalk or limit line before the light turned red, it is entirely legal. The officer must have a clear, unobstructed view, and unless he is positioned right at the intersection or on a cross street, it is unlikely that his view is completely unobstructed by other waiting vehicles.

"Here, I approached the intersection at a safe and reasonable speed, and proceeded through the yellow light, which according to VC§21452, is entirely legal. The officer who issued me the citation was on the street I turned onto and was issuing a ticket to another motorist. The officer was not looking directly at my car when I drove through the yellow light. The officer likely only glanced up as I was completing the turn at which time the light had already turned to red.

"In a criminal proceeding, 'the burden of proving the defendant's guilt beyond a reasonable doubt is upon the state' (Cal. Penal Code Sec. 1096) and this being a criminal proceeding, the burden is the same. In order to judge that I had committed any infraction, the officer would have needed a clear line of sight. In this case my guilt or innocence will depend on whether the front of my vehicle was behind or past the limit line when the light turned red. In order to gather evidence against me for use in judging my guilt or innocence, the officer needed to have a clear, unobstructed line of sight to the limit line and the front of my vehicle passing over this limit line.

"Here, the weather was gray so visibility was not at maximum and the officer's attention was not focused only on my car as I approached the limit line and then ultimately turned and he was in no position to judge when exactly the front of my car passed over the limit line. Admittedly the light may have turned red while I was completing my turn but I maintain that my car passed over the limit line PRIOR to the light turning red and the officer cannot prove otherwise as he was not facing my car at the instant I crossed the limit line.

"Given these facts a rational trier of fact could reasonably find that the officer did not have a clear line of sight to the limit line and without that clear, unobstructed line of sight the officer is without sufficient evidence to convict me."

Conclusion
While not every ticket is dismissed, fortunately this ticket was dismissed. Within six weeks the client received the letter from the court stating that the red light ticket had been 100% dismissed. No points were added to her driving record, the fines disappeared, and the client's bail amount would be returned! In addition, this client had the benefit of not having to go to court, or taking time off work, didn't have to wait in any lines at the post office and did not have to appear before a judge!

Governments need money to operate. Officers give out tickets to generate money for the city, local and state governments. The true cost of this traffic ticket could have been almost $2,000 when you take into account the cost of insurance over a 3-year period and the cost of the ticket. Fortunately you don't have to contribute to the government's coffers if you feel that you were unjustly issued a traffic ticket. You can do something about it as this client did. And most importantly it doesn't have to break up your marriage!!!

Case Study # 14—Bad Luck. Period.

Circumstances

While Mr. Michaels was driving through the desert, in the middle of the night, on a busy two lane highway, his wife, who had recently given birth, unexpectedly began to experience heavy menstrual bleeding. In this case, it was not as if Mr. Michaels could run to the local convenience store to pick up the necessary feminine products because they were in the middle of nowhere. Talk about bad luck.

His wife was panicking, which in turn made him panic, and worry about her health. At a loss over what to do, Mr. Michaels sped up to get his wife to a rest area where she could at least make do with whatever they had with them.

No big surprise, Mr. Michaels was nabbed by a CHP officer. The officer claimed he had been driving in the opposite direction and that Mr. Michaels had been clocked by radar but Mr. Michaels didn't think it was even possible to shoot radar while driving so he decided he needed to fight this ticket.

Solution

With a little more than a month remaining before the due date for his ticket Mr. Michaels brought his case to TicketBust.com. The type of ticket Mr. Michaels received, though unique to Mr. Michaels (who didn't know the first place to start with dealing with it), wasn't at all unique to TicketBust.com consultants.

The solution for Mr. Michaels' ticket was simple. The written declaration prepared for him by his TicketBust.com consultant addressed the known issues arising when radar is used when moving to discount the credibility of this method, and the many factors that could have negatively impacted the officer's ability to obtain a clear line of sight to Mr. Michaels' vehicle including the limited visibility (on account of it being dark), the heavy amount of traffic, and the distance that was between Mr. Michaels and the officer (on account on them being on opposite sides of the highway). All of these factors were brought up in order to create reasonable doubt that the officer actually clocked Mr. Michaels at the cited speed.

Conclusion
Mr. Michaels actions in picking up speed were out of necessity as he was overwhelmed with worry about his wife's condition, not out of ignorance of the law. He felt strongly the ticket was unwarranted given all the circumstances and with the help of TicketBust.com his ticket was dismissed.

Case Study #15–Slow Talking, Slow Walking Stan

Circumstances

This is a personal story. All my friends know what I do for a living and many of them didn't believe that I could actually help them successfully fight and dismiss a traffic ticket. That is, until Stan received a traffic ticket.

Every day that ends in a "Y" (that would mean everyday); I would make the journey to my local Starbucks for a cup of coffee and more importantly to shoot the sh*t with a bunch of old men. Hanging out at my local Starbucks is sort of like a combination of the television shows *Cheers*, where everyone knows your name, and *Seinfeld*, a show about nothing. Most of our time is spent arguing about who is right or wrong on a topic (Little Arnie always thinks he's right) or making fun of each other, like Slow Talking, Slow Walking Stan.

Well one day Slow Talking, Slow Walking Stan came to Starbucks and said "Steve, you'll never believe this. I got a speeding ticket for going 85 mph in a 70 mph zone on my way back from Palm Springs." Knowing Stan and knowing how he can't do anything fast, I thought there's no way in hell that he could have received a speeding ticket. Stan's the type of guy that will take 20 minutes to tell someone how he tied his shoes that morning; most people can say this in one sentence, but not Stan. So I said to Stan, "No possible way that you received a speeding ticket. Let me see that." Then I told Stan, "I want you to take a chance here. I'll fight your ticket for you for free. I'm not going to charge you and I am guaranteeing you that I will get it dismissed." Stan went into deep thought, because he does nothing fast, and after about 15 minutes of contemplation, he said "You're on."

Solution

First thing we did was have Stan come into the office, there was no way I was going to sit and listen to his whole story during a cup of coffee, it would take three cups of coffee, a bagel and a banana before Stan was done talking.

Stan arrived at my office and we began to go through a series of questions with him so that we could gather the information we needed to do our preliminary research. Stan was accused of violating California Vehicle Code Section 22356(b). This section states:

> 22356. (a) Whenever the Department of Transportation, after consultation with the Department of the California Highway Patrol, determines upon the basis of an engineering and traffic survey on existing highway segments, or upon the basis of appropriate design standards and projected traffic volumes in the case of newly constructed highway segments, that a speed greater than 65 miles per hour would facilitate the orderly movement of vehicular traffic and would be reasonable and safe upon any state highway, or portion thereof, that is otherwise subject to a maximum speed limit of 65 miles per hour, the Department of Transportation, with the approval of the Department of the California Highway Patrol, may declare a higher maximum speed of 70 miles per hour for vehicles not subject to Section 22406, and shall cause appropriate signs to be erected giving notice thereof. The Department of Transportation shall only make a determination under this section that is fully consistent with, and in full compliance with, federal law.
>
> (b) No person shall drive a vehicle upon that highway at a speed greater than 70 miles per hour, as posted.

Allegedly the officer said he was going over 100 mph, however he only issued the ticket for 85 mph. Stan must have worn him down while talking on the side of the rode about nothing more than how many times his tires would have to rotate to go that fast and the officer just couldn't bear to listen to anything else that Slow Walking Slow Talking Stan had to say, so 85 mph it was.

On November 15, 2011 at approximately 8:27 am, Stan was issued the citation. He recalled that day he was traveling east on the 10 Freeway in moderate traffic. The weather was clear at the time, and he was driving at a speed which was reasonable and prudent, having due regard for weather, visibility, traffic, and the surface and width of the roadway. He was traveling at a controlled speed which was in no way unsafe for the roadway on which he was traveling and out of habit, he made regular and frequent checks of the speedometer.

Stan stated that the officer claims to have clocked his vehicle at 85+ mph. There are a number of factors, including the fact that there was a significant distance and other cars in between Stan and the officer who was positioned in a deep white sand trench/ditch on the center median, sufficient to have prevented the officer from being able to obtain an accurate reading of Stan's speed.

Conclusion
Stan received his ticket on November 15, 2011. We completed his Trial by Written Declaration on December 15, 2011 and sent it to the Banning Court House. The ticket wasn't due until January 25, 2012 but we always like to get our documentation to the court as soon as possible. On February 8, 2012 Stan called me; unfortunately (actually fortunately in my case) I could not answer the phone so he left a message. Ok he didn't just leave a message; he wasted about 10 minutes talking about his ticket and then finally said the ticket was DISMISSED.

But there's more to this story. When the court renders a decision on a case, they send you out a decision notice called "Notice of Decision." On this notice it will say if you are guilty or if the traffic ticket is dismissed. It's very clear. It even states if you will be getting a refund because your ticket was dismissed or if you owe more money because you were found guilty.

Stan received his Decision Notice in the mail on February 8, 2012. Now he took a look at it and for whatever reason just didn't understand it so he called up another one of the morning Starbucks guys, Mark. Now Mark's the type of guy who has a story for everything and knows everyone. If you've done something, he's done it better or if you know someone, he does too, but Mark's a good guy. So Stan said to Mark, "I received this letter in the mail from the court but don't know what it means." Mark told Stan to read it to him, so Stan did. "It says, …Your case has been dismissed and your bail in the amount of $244 will be returned to you." Mark then said, "You big dummy, your traffic ticket was dismissed." Okay, there were a few more choice words but we'll leave that out of this story.

Bottom line is Slow Talking, Slow Walking Stan's traffic ticket was dismissed and he was very happy about. We have a few billboards along the 10 freeway around the Palm Springs area and now every time Stan drives by he looks up at those TicketBust.com billboards and smiles and continues on his drive safely, but knowing that if he does receive a traffic ticket, TicketBust.com is on his side.

There is an aftermath to Stan's story. Now because of helping Stan get out of a ticket, everyone I know that receives a traffic ticket wants me to help them too. Unfortunately I'm not the type of guy that charges his friends so I've created a lot of extra work, but it gives the guys at Starbucks one more thing to talk about.

Case Study # 16–The Police Referral

Circumstances

Many of our clients come to TicketBust.com as a result of a referral. You may be surprised to hear some referrals are even from police officers. Go figure.

One such client, Mr. Wallace who got ticketed by California Highway Patrol out in Barstow, California, was referred to us by one of his buddies (CHP? You guessed it).

Solution

We did an over the phone consultation with Mr. Wallace, got the details about what happened, and got a copy of his ticket which showed the officer made a glaring error. Mr. Wallace had been driving in clear weather, in a flashy silver Mercedes Benz, and was caught coming over the hill while traveling with a pack of cars, but the officer forgot to put how fast he was going! Mr. Wallace said the officer had appeared to be deep in conversation with another officer at the time he passed by and was apparently still distracted when he wrote up the citation since he failed to write down Mr. Wallace's approximate speed.

Mr. Wallace had that going for him as well as the fact his vehicle was not the only vehicle within the officer's range. He was traveling with a group of cars and there were several cars behind him as well as cars spread out amongst the lanes. He was traveling in the slow lane and was passed by a car before coming over the hill where the officer was situated. The officer's radar would have picked up the speed of this faster moving car as he crested the hill, but since he was on the other side of the hill he could not see that the car had passed him and thus would not have known that his vehicle was not the faster moving vehicle in range. The common problem with radar units is the radar beams are not tight and narrow but rather spread out and not only bounce off the target vehicle but also all other vehicles within range allowing for the target to be misidentified. All together, we felt his chances were good.

Conclusion

It usually takes about 60-90 days for the court to return a Trial by Written Declaration decision. It sometimes only takes 30 days but it's rare. For Mr. Wallace it only took about a month to receive a dismissal and a refund of over $200.

California Highway Patrol officers recommending TicketBust.com for busting tickets issued by THE CALIFORNIA HIGHWAY PATROL, talk about ironic we know. But good for us. And turned out well for Mr. Wallace in this case too.

Case Study #17–Don't Believe The Radar (Police Radar Tactics Don't Always Work)

There are many uses for radar in our society, from aircraft, and armed forces, to meteorologists, satellites and many others. Most uses of radar are appreciated and do not put the fear of God in the average person. However, there is one use of radar that can even make a grown man shake, sweat and become very nervous: police using radar to detect your speed and issue you a ticket.

Police use radar for the specific purpose of detecting how fast you're moving. The radar uses radio waves to detect how fast you are moving. It accomplishes this by sending out a burst of high-frequency radio waves and then listens for the echo once the waves hit your car and then measures the time it takes for those waves to arrive.

So what happens if the radar hits the wrong car or the officer doesn't have a clear line of sight on your car or even if you are traveling uphill or downhill? All this can affect the radar results and can render a ticket invalid.

Circumstances
In October 2009, Mr. Boar from Buena Park, CA received his first traffic violation, it was a speeding ticket. Mr. Boar is a commercial driver with a Class A license. Mr. Boar came to TicketBust.com with only one thing in mind, "I can't let my employer know that I received a traffic ticket." We assured Mr. Boar, that we were aware of his position as a commercial driver and that his job depended on having a clean driving record. We also told him not to worry and reassured him that we deal with this situation all the time. Mr. Boar told us that the officer nailed him on radar and he was terrified that meant that they had him dead to rights.

Mr. Boar told us the following:

> "On the day I was issued the citation, I was driving westbound on SR-91 amongst moderate traffic. The weather was clear and it was easy to see the roadway and

the traffic. Overall, I was driving at a speed that was reasonable or prudent having due regard for weather, visibility, the traffic and the surface and width of the roadway. I was heading up a slight incline (where I necessarily had to apply the gas to make it uphill). I came over the crest and while applying the brakes (takes a minute for the truck to slow down after coming over a crest), immediately observed what appeared to be an accident. There were two officers pulled over on the right hand side of the freeway (on a very narrow shoulder) and there was a medium duty (Bobcat) truck pulled over as well. This distracted me while I was applying the Retarder and Jake Brake to slow the truck down, and I took my eyes off the speedometer momentarily."

As Mr. Boar describes, the officers were about 7-9 seconds (approximately based on traveling at 55 mph) past the crest of the hill, parked dangerously close to the right lane of the freeway. Mr. Boar was concerned that there was an accident and concerned that he may get too close to them, so all of his attention was focused on the officers. To his surprise, one of the officers began waving at him. Mr. Boar complied and pulled over, although he was not sure why, as he did not feel his speed was excessive. He pulled over to the side and the younger officer walked up to his truck and said the other (senior) officer had clocked him on radar at 65 mph. Shortly thereafter, Mr. Boar was cited for violating California Vehicle Code section 22406 (a) - Maximum Speed for Designated Vehicles .

According to DMV this violation's description follows for VC-Section 22406 Maximum Speed for Designated Vehicles:

> 22406. No person may drive any of the following vehicles on a highway at a speed in excess of 55 miles per hour:
>
> > (a) A motor truck or truck tractor having three or more axles or any motor truck or truck tractor drawing any other vehicle.

(b) A passenger vehicle or bus drawing any other vehicle.

(c) A schoolbus transporting any school pupil.

(d) A farm labor vehicle when transporting passengers.

(e) A vehicle transporting explosives.

(f) A trailer bus, as defined in Section 636.

Solution

Mr. Boar was a keen, professional driver and went to the internet for help. As are so many of TicketBust.com's clients, Mr. Boar was a truck driver and relied on his exceptional driving record in order to maintain his employee status.

In order to develop a proper defense for Mr. Boar, we keyed in on several issues related to how the officer measured Mr. Boar 's speed:

- It is necessary for the officer's declaration to contain substantial evidence that the speed measurement was obtained in compliance with accepted operating procedures;

- The officer's declaration must contain substantial evidence that the radar speed measurement was obtained in compliance with accepted operating procedures which the officer must show by establishing that:

  - The radar was operating properly;

  - The accuracy was verified with an appropriate method both before and after shift;

- The operator (officer) was properly qualified and trained;

- There was a visual observation and initial estimate of the apparent excessive speed independent of any reading by the radar unit;

- The reading obtained by the radar unit was reasonably close to the visual estimation.

- It is necessary for the officer to prove successful completion of Radar Operator Training Requirements.

- Subparagraph (A) of CVC§40802 sets forth certain requirements of the training of an officer using radar to measure speed of an accused. Subparagraph (A) appears under speed trap law, but the same standards would apply whether the alleged violation is of the basic speed law (where there is a prima facie speed limit) or maximum speed law. These requirements are foundational requirements which must be established before the officer's evidence of radar should be accepted and considered.

There are also several other factors that we brought to the courts attention when submitting Mr. Boar's Trial by Written Declaration to the court:

- It is necessary for the radar that the officer used to have met or exceeded the minimum operation standards of the National Highway Traffic Safety Administration;

- It is necessary for the officer to have conducted an equipment accuracy check both at shift start and shift end on the date the equipment was used to obtain a speed measurement;

- It is necessary for the officer's declaration to contain substantial evidence of the officer's training in the use of visual estimations of speed;

- It is necessary for the officer to have had a clear line of sight on the day of the issuance of the citation;

- Conditions or factors which prevented officer from having a clear line of sight to the cited vehicle on the day of the issuance of the citation including:

  - Less than ideal road conditions

  - Limited visibility factor

  - Less than ideal traffic conditions

  - Absence of relatively close distance

  - Obstructions present

Conclusion
In Mr. Boar's case, we concluded the following:

- Based on the location where the officer was when Mr. Boar first saw him, and given the above mentioned factors at the time, the officer could not have had a clear line of sight to Mr. Boar's vehicle. The officer could not have reasonably obtained any measurement from his vehicle through use of any method (whether it be visual, radar, pacing, or otherwise) without a clear line of sight.

- Moreover, we asked the court to also consider that the officer's method for estimating Mr. Boar's speed is a method which is not completely free from error. Given this, and given the fact that without a clear line of sight the officer could not have accurately identified his traveling speed, a rational trier of fact could not reasonably find that the officer was able to make both an accurate initial visual estimate of the speed prior to the reading by the radar unit and a subsequent reading by the radar unit all with an obstructed line of sight. We asked the court to dismiss the citation in the interest of justice.

Mr. Boar was found not guilty and his bail was returned, but more importantly, his driving record remained spotless!

Technology is great, but technology just for the sake of technology is pointless and in the wrong hands can be destructive and negatively affect the lives of many individuals. If Mr. Boar was found guilty, he would have lost his job and his family would endure grave hardships. It is imperative that the people using technology, in this case a radar gun to estimate speed, understand how to properly use and maintain the device so that they do not issue erroneous traffic tickets and affect the lives of countless law-abiding drivers on our California Highways.

Now go hit the road, drive safely and if you do get a speeding ticket where the officer used a radar gun you now have the knowledge and insight to understand that all officers with radar guns are not created equally.

Case Study #18 – Red Light Camera Victory

Cameras are an integral part of our lives. Just about every person owns and uses a camera, whether it be a camera phone or actual camera. And if not for cameras we wouldn't be able to easily preserve cherished memories. At first thought it's hard to think of anything negative about a camera, right? Well, there is one type of camera that has a lot of people pissed off; the dreaded red light camera.

Red light cameras were put in use in the United States as early as the 1990's and there is still much controversy about them. The thought of being under surveillance when passing through a camera enforced intersection is upsetting. The thought of police being able to issue you a ticket for something they didn't see with their own eyes infuriates people. And actually getting a ticket in the mail with a picture of your smiling face and a $400 plus fine attached, drives most people up the wall.

So what's the deal with these red light cameras then? With so much controversy why are they still in use? There are many theories. Supporters say they increase safety and decrease accidents caused by people running red lights. Opposers say they actually increase rear end collisions because people will prematurely slam on their brakes at camera enforced intersections and/or that the primary use is to generate revenue not to increase safety. Court cases challenging the validity of evidence gathered by red light cameras have returned verdicts both in favor and in opposition of the red light cameras. One thing's for sure; we are seeing more and more judges rule in favor of the motorist ticketed.

Take this case for example:

Circumstances
Mr. Guerrero received a red light photo ticket in the mail from the Riverside Superior Court stating he had to appear in court. He was in his personal vehicle when the incident occurred but on the ticket the space for commercial driver was marked. Commercial drivers are not permitted in California to take traffic school to keep

points from affecting their license and Mr. Guerrero feared how this ticket would affect his license and, effectively, his ability to earn a living.

Mr. Guerrero began surfing the web searching for answers to help him understand why he had received the ticket in the mail and how to take care of it.

He felt fortunate to have come across www.combatesuticket.com (the TicketBust.com Latin division which caters to California's Hispanic market allowing the Latin community in our state to work with us in their native language). Having assisted thousands of drivers with red light camera tickets just like his, we felt confident we could help Mr. Guerrero achieve a positive outcome.

Solution

- Mr. Guerrero informed us of three key facts he remembered from the day of the incident:

- He neared the intersection as the light was green and when the light turned yellow, he felt he was too near the limit line to stop safely before entering the intersection;

- Cars were following closely behind him and he felt slamming on the brakes at the last minute would cause an accident;

- He hadn't seen a steady red signal prior to crossing the limit line.

We found out the following which we felt applied to Mr. Guerrero's set of circumstances:

- Per California Law, Vehicle Code section 21452 - a driver is not required to stop for a yellow light but are rather merely warned that a red light is to follow;

- Considering the rule adopted in *People v. Ausen* (1940) 40 Cal.App.2d Supp. 831(where the court held that they do not regard traffic signals as: "a rule absolute under all circumstances" or an absolute rule under all circumstances), the court should apply a similar rule and grant leniency given the fact Mr. Guerrero was unable to stop safely due to the risk of being rear ended;

- The violation code he was cited for, California Vehicle Code section 21453 (a), stated: "A driver facing a steady circular red signal alone shall stop at a marked limit line...," so the ticket should not have been issued since there was not a "steady red" signal showing before he crossed the limit line.

Upon further investigation we also discovered there may be an issue with the contract the City of Corona (from where the ticket was issued) had with the camera company (called Redflex) that could help Mr. Guerrero win his case:

> California law (Vehicle Code section 21455.5 (g)) says "a contract between a governmental agency and a manufacturer or supplier of automated enforcement equipment may not include a provision for payment of compensation to the manufacturer or supplier based on the number of citations generated or percentage of revenue generated as a result of use of the equipment."

In this case, we found the City of Corona's agreement with the camera operator, Redflex included payment language connecting payment to the operator to revenue generated by the system, which we felt to be in direct violation of California Vehicle Code 21455.5 (g)(1). The purpose of the statute is logically to avoid an incentive to the camera operator, as a neutral evaluator of evidence, to increase the number of citations issued and paid through use of the equipment.

We presented the following issues in Mr. Guerrero's declaration to the court:

- Mr. Guerrero was not legally required to stop when the light turned yellow;

- Mr. Guerrero could not have stopped for the yellow light even if he had wanted to due to the risk of causing and being involved in an accident;

- There was no steady red light visible to Mr. Guerrero prior to the time he crossed the limit line;

- The contract between the City of Corona and the camera operator unlawfully allowed for payments to be based in effect on the numbers of citations generated, and it in effect provides direct financial incentive to the camera operator to manipulate the photographic evidence before forwarding them to the city in order to provide the city with photographic incidents from which tickets could be generated.

Conclusion

Many people believe that red light camera tickets are tough to beat and the only way you can win is if the officer doesn't show up in court or if you are contesting the ticket using a Trial by Written Declaration, if the officer fails to respond. Mr. Guerrero is living proof that it is possible to be victorious in a red light camera ticket dispute.

The court received Mr. Guerrero's request for Trial by Written Declaration in late December 2011. The court followed procedures by then notifying the officer the ticket was being contested and to file his response, called an Officer's Declaration, by the end of January, 2012.

The officer DID respond, and the judge reviewed both Mr. Guerrero's declaration as well as the officer's and still ruled in favor of Mr. Guerrero.

In Mr. Guerrero's case, the ticket was not only expensive, but also threatened his ability to earn a living since the ticket, if upheld, would have resulted in another point being added to Mr. Guerrero's driving record. Unfortunately, not all red light cameras are operated in compliance with the law and sometimes a ticket is issued when it really should not have been, as was the case for Mr. Guerrero.

A little extra effort into finding out which company operates the red light camera system in the city in which you were cited and what the contract says about how the city pays the camera company, combined with a well thought out defense for a red light camera ticket can return positive results.

Case Study #19–I Never Thought I Could Get A Ticket On A Jet Ski

"Thinking is the hardest work there is which is probably why so few engage in it"
–Henry Ford (American industrialist and pioneer of the assembly-line production method, 1863-1947)

Circumstances
Everyone likes to have a little fun and so did Mr. Long from Diamond Bar, California. On a hot day in September, Mr. Long decided that it was time to learn how to jet ski. Mr. Long had never been jet skiing before and thought that this would be the perfect day to learn how. So Mr. Long headed out to Lake Perris.

I know what most of you are thinking now. You're thinking: "Oh great! Another story about how someone was speeding in their car. How typical! But I'm so tired of reading about your run-of-the-mill speeding stories where TicketBust.com gets the ticket dismissed as usual. I want something different, I want something exciting and more interesting than just a typical speeding ticket."

Well we have the answer with this one. Yes, Mr. Long was cited for speeding, but not for speeding in his car. Mr. Long was cited for speeding while riding on a JET SKI. Yes, you read that correctly, Mr. Long received a speeding ticket for going 20 mph in a 5 mph zone. Mr. Long never thought about the speed laws while operating a jet ski, he never even knew that there were any such laws.

I bet you never thought you could get a ticket for speeding on a jet ski, especially when you're just trying to have a little fun. But you can. It happened to Mr. Long and it can happen to you, too. Luckily, these tickets can be contested too.

So here's the situation straight from Mr. Long's mouth:

> "On the day I was issued the citation at issue in this case, I was jet skiing for the very first time, in Lake Perris. At the

time there was a very minimal amount of water traffic and there were no people in the water and no other jet skis nearby. The weather was clear that day and I had very good visibility while riding the jet ski. I was riding at a speed which was reasonable and prudent, having due regard for weather, visibility, and traffic in the water. While riding the jet ski, the citing officer approached in a boat. I was riding at a controlled speed which was in no way unsafe for the existing conditions at the time and at no time did I feel I was riding at 20 mph in the 5 mph zone."

Solution
The successful prosecution of any speeding violation involving a jet ski requires, among other things, that all elements of the alleged offense be established. The officer must first and foremost:

- Establish and identify the driver of the alleged offending jet ski;

- Establish that the jet ski in question was the jet ski from which the speed measurement was obtained;

- Identify the posted speed limit in force at the location (here Lake Perris) in question;

- Establish that the violator's speed was unreasonable and unsafe given the conditions at the time of the violation, or otherwise excessive.

In California the defendant does not bear any burden of proof in defending his or herself against a charge for violating a posted speed because pursuant to Cal. Penal Code §1096, the People must prove their case beyond a reasonable doubt. The People, in this case, will seek to disprove Mr. Long's innocence through the declaration by the police officer. The successful prosecution of any speeding violation involving a jet ski requires, among other things, that all elements of the alleged offense be established.

The officer indicated on the citation that radar was not used. The officer could only be relying on a visual observation of Mr. Long's speed since there was no opportunity for the officer to pace Mr. Long's jet ski in order to obtain a measurement of his speed that way.

A subjective visual estimation of speed is the least credible type of method an officer may use to assess a jet ski's speed. Proof of the officer's actual training records containing information regarding the accuracy of the officer's visual estimations of speed is lacking.

Based on where the officer was when he first saw Mr. Long, the officer could not have accurately identified traveling speed, especially not without the use of radar or a pacing method to verify that his visual speed estimation was correct.

There is also no proof that Mr. Long's speed had endangered the safety of persons or property and the officer has not established that the cited speed was unreasonable for the conditions existing at the time of the alleged violation.

Conclusion
Alright, I bet you can guess what the outcome of this case was. That's correct, this ticket was dismissed, no points went on his driving record and Mr. Long's bail was returned to him in full.

This just goes to show you that whether you're driving an 18-wheeler for a living or are just driving to a recreational destination, like a lake, you can drive safely and get there without receiving a traffic ticket. However, if you think that just because you've made it to your destination you can relax and not worry about some other type of ticket, you are mistaken. As the case with Mr. Long shows he never thought that he would receive a traffic ticket just by having some recreational fun on a lake.

Traffic tickets can be received on just about any type of moving vehicle including a bicycle, motorcycle, ATV, jet ski, speed boat or other boat, plane, and even a run-of-the-mill ordinary automobile.

So it is wise to always be aware of the laws of the road or in this case the lake, and to drive within those laws and for your safety and the safety of others.

Case Study #20–Attack of the Killer Sheep

Circumstances
LOOK OUT, SHEEP!

Ms. Bradford narrowly missed getting into an accident by darting into the next lane to avoid the sheep staring right at her, readying itself to jump from the bed of the tiny pick-up truck which had suddenly cut her off.

Ms. Bradford was disgruntled, and rightfully so! You would think she'd be praised for her quick reflexes and good defensive driving skills instead of punished by a ticket for an unsafe lane change. She went out searching for help and stumbled upon TicketBust.com. She submitted an email to us, and her message was clear cut and simple. "It's a long story can you contact me to talk about it?" We did, and this is what we found:

The California DMV states this about her ticket:

VC - Section - 21658 "Laned Roadways":

21658. Whenever any roadway has been divided into two or more clearly marked lanes for traffic in one direction, the following rules apply:

> A vehicle shall be driven as nearly as practical entirely within a single lane and shall not be moved from the lane until such movement can be made with reasonable safety.

> Official signs may be erected directing slow-moving traffic to use a designated lane or allocating specified lanes to traffic moving in the same direction, and drivers of vehicles shall obey the directions of the traffic device.

The law seemed pretty cut and dry to her and she didn't feel she had a chance since there weren't any exceptions to the law. We thought, and found, differently.

Even if there is no exception specifically laid out in the law for emergency circumstances, as there is for cell phone use while driving, an emergency situation can be used as a defense in many cases.

When the court is presented with an emergency excuse it will judge whether or not the severity of the emergency situation justified the action taken that resulted in violating the law.

Emergency excuses must be used with common sense and care because with this type of defense you are essentially stating that you violated the law but only due to emergency circumstances beyond your control. It can be more damaging to your case admitting guilt to violating the law if your "emergency" excuse is not something the court would consider a true emergency.

If you were in danger of imminent harm and had to change lanes to avoid danger, this could be considered a true emergency. If, however, you made a quick lane change while in a hurry to reach a rest stop because your stomach hurt, while it may seem like a big deal to you, it most likely would not be a justifiable excuse in the court's eyes because you were in no real danger, you were just in discomfort.

Conclusion
We felt Ms. Bradford's situation certainly constituted a true emergency given the fact that she was in danger of colliding with the truck that had cut sharply in front of her and further in danger of having her windshield crushed by the loose sheep.

Combining case law with Ms. Bradford's great account of the factual happenings on the day she got the citation, TicketBust.com was able to prepare for Ms. Bradford a successful case for dismissal.

Sadly though, now traumatized after narrowly missing being pummeled by the rogue sheep...Ms. Bradford suffers from many a sleepless night, no longer able to find solace in envisioning an endless series of identical white sheep jumping over a fence.

They Tried But Didn't Get Off

Now that you've heard about the ones that "got off," how about the ones that didn't get off? Over the last eight years and over 50,000 traffic ticket cases, we have heard some wild excuses. Remember the one when you were in school about the dog eating your homework? Well, we've heard the same type of lame excuses about why someone was speeding or had to run a red light.

I think the best thing to remember is there is no excuse for breaking the law. I might also mention that there is no excuse for not knowing the law or being ignorant of the law. For example, not knowing that the speed limit was 65 mph or not knowing that a red light means stop in this country really won't work as a proper defense.

Ok, now that I've given you a little background here, take a read though these excuses. I think you'll be able to understand why these people didn't "get off"!!!

Excuse #1: Overactive Bladder

"I have a bladder condition and had to go really bad!"

Ms. Nelly was cited for violating CVC§22349 for speeding on the freeway in a 65 mph zone. Ever go on a long road trip as a kid and be forced to hold it because dad wanted to beat traffic? Just about anyone can attest to how uncomfortable it is to have to "hold it," however, having to go "really badly" is not something the court would readily dismiss a ticket for.

Excuse #2: Intoxicated Patient

"I was transporting an intoxicated patient who kept vomiting in the car. I sped up to drop her off fast because it was raining and I couldn't roll down the windows!"

Mrs. Jones was cited for violating CVC§22356 by exceeding the maximum posted speed limit of 70 mph. True, the smell in the car that day must have been overwhelming but her speeding excuse apparently did not present a true emergency in the eyes of the court.

Excuse #3: Stiff Neck

"I had to change lanes to exit the freeway but I couldn't turn all the way around to check for traffic because my neck was too stiff."

Mr. Kent was cited for violating CVC§21658 after making an unsafe lane change. It's true Mr. Kent's neck really was sore. He even had a note from his chiropractor backing up his story. The court did not dismiss this ticket as he had nearly mowed down a police officer on a motorcycle (the very officer who issued him the ticket) while changing lanes!

Excuse #4: Choking on Chips

"My mom was eating potato chips in the car and started coughing. I sped up because I thought she was choking!"

Ms. Logan was cited for violating CVC§22349 by going above the state's Maximum Speed Law. Now you're probably thinking this had to present a valid defense, but she did not call 911, did not request the officer to call for medical help, and her mom had already stopped coughing by the time the officer spotted them. This too did not present a true emergency and the court was unforgiving.

Excuse #5: IBS

"I was having an episode of Irritable Bowel Syndrome causing me to be extremely anxious and focused on finding a gas station or rest stop."

Mrs. Pat was cited for exceeding the state's maximum speed of 65 mph for freeways. While her condition must have made driving in the car quite uncomfortable, the court did not find sufficient justification for speeding up to 72 mph in a 65 mph zone.

Excuse #6: Bad Headache

"I had a bad migraine and was just trying to get home to take some aspirin."

Ms. Joy was cited for violating CVC§21453. The court did not find this situation warranted blowing through a red light (it didn't help the officer had been right behind her when she did it).

Compare the above cases to this case out of Manchester, New Hampshire. The defendant, named John Coughlin, was found not guilty of excessive speeding (over 100 mph) to get his pregnant wife to the hospital. The difference? The judge was able to take into account that he called 911 to report his wife was having a baby, and on top of that he was given a police escort at 3:00 in the morning to the hospital, where minutes after arriving his wife gave birth to their son. Clearly this presented a "true emergency" to the court.

Excuse #7: Rude Officer

"The officer was in a bad mood and out to get me."

Mrs. David was cited for multiple violations resulting from speeding, unsafe lane changes, unsafe turning movements, failing to signal for a turn, no registration in vehicle, and failing to notify the DMV of an address change. She stuck to her story that she hadn't done anything wrong and that the officer had simply been picking on her. If you read our last book you know by now how we feel about bad mouthing the officer to the judge. Never have we seen this result in a favorable judgment, and this situation was no different.

There are other means to complain about an unprofessional officer, like filing a grievance report with a superior officer at the police department where your citing officer is stationed. It is not proper to complain to the judge about the officer as it does not help establish to the judge why you are not guilty.

Excuse #8: Can't Speed in a Prius

"I drive a Toyota Prius Hybrid vehicle and can't go that fast, plus why would I speed when I obviously like to conserve fuel."

Ms. Dox was accused of violating California Vehicle Code section 22350 by accelerating to 55 mph in a 40 mph zone, and she was adamant about using her excuse as an angle to fight her ticket. See the problem here? If Ms. Dox is arguing that her Prius "can't go that fast" then why do we see these cars on the freeway where you have to go 65 mph? Needless to say, this excuse did not work for Ms. Dox.

Compare this case to cases involving truck drivers in semi-trucks. Many of these trucks are "governed" to not go faster than, say, 62 mph. When a commercial driver is traveling on a flat highway in a truck governed at 62 mph, but is ticketed by an officer for going 68 mph, it can easily be argued that the officer was wrong. The "my car can't go that fast" argument is not going to work in most cases involving regular passenger cars that have a speedometer with a needle that goes up to 100 mph +, because it's entirely possible for a judge to believe you were, in fact, "going that fast."

Excuse #9: Broken Speedometer

"I figured out my cars speedometer wasn't working properly. Upon having my brakes changed, my mechanic found a fault on my speedometer wire so my speedometer had not been working properly."

Mr. Tran was cited for speeding under California Vehicle Code 22356, and you're probably thinking this should have been a slam dunk win since he had documentation proving his speedometer had been broken. Why didn't this work you ask? Well, we will talk about the broken speedometer issue later in our "Truth or Fiction" section but what we will tell you now is this:

For the broken speedometer excuse to have any chance of success, the difference between the speed limit and the speed the officer said you were going has got to be equal to or less than the number your mechanic says your speedometer was off by. In the case of Mr. Tran, his speedometer was only off by 5-6 mph while his speed was in excess of 26 mph of the posted speed limit.

Excuse #10: DWP (Driving While Pretty)

"I'm a young, petite, attractive woman, with red hair and green eyes, driving a convertible with the top down, who wouldn't want to pull me over."

Ms. Carrol was stopped on the freeway by an officer for violating California Vehicle Code 22349 (a) by driving in excess of 65 mph. She was convinced that the only reason the officer had stopped her was because she was pretty and wanted to talk to her and she even sent the court a color photograph so the judge could see for himself.

Of all the crazy excuses we've heard over the years, this is definitely at the top of the list. And, by the way, don't bother trying to get out of a ticket using this excuse; we can assure you it didn't work.

Traffic Ticket Deal or No Deal

Unless you just skipped to this section, you've already read about the people who "got off" and got their traffic ticket dismissed. Then you read about some of the crazy excuses people used and why their traffic ticket didn't get dismissed and why they didn't "get off."

Now let's put your knowledge to the test. If you were provided two situations, would you be able to pick the driver that "Got Off"? Ok then, lets find out.

Here we go with Traffic Ticket: Deal or No Deal.

1. Deal or No Deal: Driver A or Driver B.

Driver A, on her way to her 18th birthday party, encountered a motorist who appeared to be driving while intoxicated. The other driver was weaving through the lanes and speeding up and slowing down erratically. She had forgotten her hands free device at home and made a call to police while holding the phone in her hand. In the midst of this she was stopped by an officer for holding a phone and talking while driving (CVC§23123).

Driver B, while driving on the eve of her 18th birthday, needed to make a call to her friends to firm up plans for the party the next day. She briefly took off her seatbelt in order to retrieve her hands free device from the glove box and made her call using it. The officer spotted her with her seatbelt off and also on the phone. He ended up giving her a warning for the seatbelt but issued the ticket for the cell phone violation.

So who do you think would Get Off, Driver A or B? **Deal** Driver A, **No Deal** Driver B. Here's why:

California enacted hands free laws years ago and unless you are using a hands free device you are not supposed to talk on the phone unless there is an emergency. Driver A did not use a hands free device but is exempted from the law because there was an emergency call being made to police. Although Driver B seemed to be in compliance by using a hands free device, she was also a minor at the time. Under California law (CVC§23124) a minor may not talk on a phone while driving even if it is being used in a hands free manner, unless the purpose is for an emergency.

2. Deal or No Deal: Driver A or Driver B.

Driver A, while in route to make a delivery, looked down to his map for directions and by the time he looked up it was too late to stop for the light. He received a red light camera ticket (CVC§21453) in the mail showing him going straight through a light that had been red for close to a full second.

Driver B, also received a red light camera ticket in the mail which showed him making a "CA rolling right" and the light had been red for less than half a second.

So who do you think would Get Off, Driver A or B? **No Deal** Driver A, **Deal** Driver B. Here's why:

True, a driver making a right hand turn on a red light can be perceived as being less of a safety hazard when compared to a driver going straight through a red light or making a left turn after a light has turned red. Driver B also had another thing going for him; the light had been red for less than half a second. Although the law does not mandate them to do so, some local governments employ grace periods of up to five-tenths of a second before their red light cameras will begin taking photographs (2002 California State Auditor Report, page 45). In fact, the Federal Highway Administration indicates that a grace period of three-tenths of a second is commonly used and that five-tenths of a second is the international standard (2002 California State Auditor Report, page 45). We have found court's are generally more lenient the shorter the late time.

3. Deal or No Deal: Driver A or Driver B.

Driver A, driving through a residential area was stopped and cited for violating California's basic speed law (CVC§22350). There was heavy traffic and a school nearby.

Driver B, same scenario but there was light traffic and no schools nearby.

So who do you think would Get Off, Driver A or B? **No Deal** Driver A **Deal** Driver B. Here's why:

California's basic speed law says: "No person shall drive a vehicle upon a highway at a speed greater than is reasonable or prudent having due regard for weather, visibility, the traffic on, and the surface and width of, the highway, and in no event at a speed which endangers the safety of persons or property." Factors the courts take into consideration when determining whether the speed was safe include the presence of pedestrians, schools, parks, driveways, weather conditions, traffic conditions, etc. Driver B had better driving conditions than Driver A including the absence of schools and only light traffic versus heavy traffic.

4. Deal or No Deal: Driver A or Driver B.

Driver A, driving on the freeway at a time when there was no traffic, failed to signal when making a lane change to exit the freeway and was cited for an unsafe lane change ticket (CVC§21658).

Driver B, had the same scenario except Driver B used his turn signal and made a quick lane change in heavy traffic, causing the car in the next lane to honk.

So who do you think would Get Off, Driver A or B? **Deal** Driver A, **No Deal** Driver B. Here's why:

California law says: "...A vehicle shall be driven as nearly as practical entirely within a single lane and shall not be moved from the lane until such movement can be made with reasonable safety." It's true that Driver A did not use a turn signal but factors the court take into consideration when determining whether the lane change was safe include the proximity of other vehicles, despite whether you used a turn signal, as this particular law states nothing about having to use a signal. Although Driver B used a turn signal and Driver A did not, Driver B is in a worse position because he cut off another car in the process of the lane change.

5. Deal or No Deal: Driver A or Driver B.

Driver A, was stopped and cited for failing to obey a "stop" sign (CVC§22450) while driving down a residential street. The officer had driven up from behind.

Driver B, same scenario except the officer was parked perpendicular to the "stop" sign (at a 90 degree angle).

So who do you think would Get Off, Driver A or B? **Deal** Driver A, **No Deal** Driver B. Here's why:

The nose of a car will elevate slightly when it comes to a complete rest and no doubt officers look for this when deciding whether or not to ticket. The only place to view this accurately is from a position that is perpendicular (at a 90 degree angle) to the vehicle at the "stop" sign. Driver A could successfully argue the officer did not have a clear line of sight from behind his vehicle to view whether he made the complete stop.

6. Deal or No Deal. Driver A or Driver B.

Driver A, was stopped for speeding (CVC§22350) while traveling home one night for doing 55 mph in a 40 mph zone. He lost his ticket and went to his court date not knowing what method the officer used to clock his speed.

Driver B, same scenario but he kept his ticket in a safe place, which noted that the officer used radar.

So who do you think would Get Off, Driver A or B? **No Deal** Driver A, **Deal** Driver B. Here's why:

To successfully fight a speeding ticket you first need to determine what method the officer used to clock your speed. An officer can clock your speed using radar or laser, can pace you or make a visual estimation, or can even use a partner who is radioed in from another location on the ground or in a plane, and this will be indicated on your ticket. You need to know what method the officer used to clock your speed so you can discount the credibility of this method. The method the officer used will determine how to fight the ticket and, like Driver A; you can't successfully fight a speeding ticket without knowing the method the officer used to clock your speed.

7. Deal or No Deal: Driver A or Driver B.

Driver A, while driving on her way home, was stopped and cited for a red light violation (CVC§21453). The officer had his motorcycle parked on the corner of the intersection closest to her.

Driver B, same scenario but the officer was driving towards her (coming from the opposite side of the intersection).

So who do you think would Get Off, Driver A or B? **No Deal** Driver A, **Deal** Driver B. Here's why:

California law says: "A driver facing a steady circular red signal alone shall stop at a marked limit line..." With these types of tickets it is your word against the officer's so you will need to create reasonable doubt as to whether the officer's observations were accurate. You can do this by showing that the officer did not have a clear line of sight to the traffic signal to see it was not a "steady circular red signal." Driver B could easily do this as the officer was not facing the same signal she was.

8. Deal or No Deal: Driver A or Driver B.

Driver A was stopped and cited for traveling at 67 MPH while driving a commercial truck which is restricted to 55 MPH on California highways (CVC§22406). He was keeping up with the flow of traffic of other trucks in the slow lane.

Driver B, same scenario but he moved out of the slow lane and was passing other vehicles.

So who do you think would Get Off, Driver A or B? **Deal** Driver A, **No Deal** Driver B. Here's why.

When it comes to a speeding ticket you have the best shot at winning if there was a lead car in the pack that is not you. Also if there are other drivers passing you, your speed will seem slower by comparison. Here Driver B was the fastest vehicle in the pack, passing other vehicles.

9. Deal or No Deal: Driver A or Driver B.

Driver A was driving when stopped by the CHP officer who had paced him. He was cited for speed over 70 mph & illegal window tint (CVC§22356 & 26708). It was a clear day, there was a lot of traffic and the area was mountainous.

Driver B, same scenario except there was no traffic and the area was flat and straight.

So who do you think would Get Off, Driver A or B? **Deal** Driver A, **No Deal** Driver B. Here's why.

When an officer follows along with your vehicle to pace you, the officer needs to be able to keep your vehicle in sight for the duration of the pace. If there is limited visibility, a lot of traffic on the road around you, or the road is hilly or curved, all of these things could affect the officer's ability to keep your car in view long enough to allow for a decent pace to be conducted. Driver B already made himself a target by having the illegal window tint and on top of that the officer could have easily paced him as it was during the day, with no traffic and along a flat, straight stretch of roadway.

10. Deal or No Deal: Driver A or Driver B.

Driver A, was ticketed for multiple violations including Speed (CVC§22350), unsafe lane change (CVC§21658), unsafe turn (CVC§22107), failure to signal (CVC§22108), no registration (CVC§4454), & failure to notify DMV of change of address (CVC§14600). Driver A felt she was wrongly ticketed but was amicable and compliant with the officer.

Driver B, same scenario except she was very upset about the ticket and let it be known to the officer. She jumped out of her car after pulling over, putting the officers on the defensive. She argued and cried while the officers questioned her and ultimately was so hysterical the police supervisor had to be called out.

So who do you think would Get Off, Driver A or B? You're probably thinking there's no way in hell either are getting off, but **Deal** Driver A, **No Deal** Driver B.

You want the officer to remember as little about you as possible so if and when it comes time to fight the ticket you will have the advantage (you may only have to worry about this one ticket, the officer may have written hundreds more by that time you go to fight it). Just like we say in our TicketBust.com Top Traffic Ticket Tips, remain calm and polite, do not get out of your vehicle unless asked, and do not do anything memorable in front of the officer. You can bet the officers remembered every little detail about Driver B's ticket and even changed their vacation schedule to make sure they were around in case she wanted to fight it.

Truth or Fiction

Everybody's heard a story or two about what is true or false regarding traffic tickets and who knows what to believe. Haven't we all been at the dinner party or having coffee with some friends and the subject of traffic tickets comes up and all of a sudden you have five experts in the room all thinking they know more than the next person about traffic tickets. Over the years this has created a lot of misinformation and myths. Some of the myths have even gone on to become modern day folklore.

So let's separate the truth from the fiction and debunk the modern day myths about getting traffic tickets and your rights after you've received a traffic ticket.

An officer can refuse to show you the radar gun.

Truth or Fiction? **Truth**.

Many times an officer will show you the radar gun upon request. Or if feeling especially generous, may show it to you unsolicited. However, your request may well be legally denied to you. The officer may feel his safety would be compromised by bringing you back to his vehicle to see the radar or may feel your safety would be compromised by having you get out to view the radar gun while high speed traffic is whizzing by.

You can't get a ticket for speeding if you're just going with the flow of traffic.

Truth or Fiction? **Fiction**.

It's a common misconception. California has a basic speed law which states you must drive at a speed which is safe for the conditions at hand. This could mean going a little slower if there is heavy traffic or inclement weather, or a bit faster so as not to impede traffic. But if everyone around you is going 50 mph and the speed limit is 35 mph, that doesn't mean you can't get a ticket for speeding.

It's a speed trap if a bunch of officers are parked at the bottom of a hill waiting to catch people speeding.

Truth or Fiction? **Fiction**.

The phrase "speed trap" gets thrown around a lot when people are angry about a ticket and feel wronged by an officer. But by definition this is not a speed trap. By definition, a speed trap is when an officer uses radar (any electronic speed measurement device) on a particular section of highway where the posted prima facie speed limit has not been justified by an engineering and traffic survey.

A Trial by Jury and a Public Defender are available to me in a traffic infraction case.

Truth or Fiction? **Fiction**.

If you ever tried to get a jury trial for your speeding ticket you probably got shot down. Sometime around 1969, California created a new way to classify the majority of traffic violations: the infraction. A person charged with an infraction is not entitled to a trial by jury or a public defender (CA Penal Code 19.6). An infraction is also not punishable by imprisonment, which is why you don't get thrown in jail for forgetting to signal.

If the officer doesn't have me sign the ticket then it isn't valid.

Truth of Fiction? **Fiction**.

If an officer forgot to have you sign your citation, it may go to show they weren't paying full attention, but by no means invalidates the ticket. Your signature only allows the officer to release you from the traffic stop without hauling you to jail. When your ticket is filed with the court and you choose not to respond based on not having signed the ticket, you will have to answer to the court. You may be charged a civil assessment penalty, get a "Failure to Appear" (a misdemeanor and probably much more serious offense than the original infraction), have a warrant put out for your arrest, and eventually your license suspended.

An officer can "hide out" or be out of plain sight while monitoring traffic.

Truth or Fiction? **Truth.**

While there may be rules in the California Vehicle Code which say an officer on duty for traffic enforcement must be in full uniform and use a distinctive painted patrol vehicle, there in nothing written as far as where an officer must stand or park while monitoring traffic.

Officers only ticket for speeding over 5 mph?

Truth or Fiction? **Fiction.**

If you've ever driven on a major California freeway in the fast lane and you don't have a lead foot, you've probably just about been run off the road. While going 5 MPH over the speed limit may be the norm for most drivers, it's still speeding! Officers absolutely can and will ticket you for driving 5 MPH over any posted speed limit. If there are bigger fish to fry in the area going faster than you, your chances of getting a ticket are probably less, but it is still an absolute possibility.

If you get a ticket in California while driving with an out of state license, there's no reason to worry because it won't affect your out of state license.

Truth or Fiction? **Fiction.**

Whether your out of state license will be affected depends on whether California notifies your home state of the violation. There is something called a "Drivers License Compact" in which most states participate (including California). Participating states report and exchange information with each other on traffic violations committed by persons who have been convicted in their state with an out of state driver's license (with the exception of Georgia, Massachusetts, Michigan, and Wisconsin, all the rest of the States are part of the compact).

Traffic School is not available after contesting a ticket through Trial by Written Declaration.

Truth or Fiction? **Fiction**.

 Under state law, there's nothing that says if you contest your traffic ticket through Trial by Declaration and are found guilty, you can't take traffic school. In general, it is up to the court's discretion to determine if you should be allowed to attend traffic school for your ticket.

Police officers don't show up in court for a red light photo ticket since the ticket is generated by a camera and not an officer.

Truth or Fiction? **Fiction**.

All red light camera tickets have a police department listed on it. The police are involved with these types of ticket and a police officer is summoned to appear in court should you choose to have a court trial and contest it.

Radar detectors are legal to have in your personal vehicle.

Truth or Fiction? **Truth**.

Radar Detectors, while they may be frowned upon by police and courts alike, are not illegal in California. In fact they are legal in most states with the exception of Virginia and Washington D.C. (as well as all Military Bases) to have in a passenger vehicle. Radar detectors are, however, illegal by Federal Law in Commercial Vehicles weighing more than 10,000 pounds. Radar jammers, on the other hand, are illegal. Section 28150 of the California Vehicle

Code says so, and if you are caught with four or more in your vehicle you are guilty of a misdemeanor!

License plate spray is legal.

Truth of Fiction? **Fiction**.

Tempted to spray your license plate with a product that's supposed to reflect the flash of a camera and avoid getting caught by a red light camera? Think again! It's illegal in California. Although vehicle code section 5201 does not specifically call out "license plate blocker spray" it does say you cannot put any product that obstructs or impairs the reading (or recognition) of a license plate by an electronic device operated by law enforcement. And, license plate blocker spray is definitely a product that impairs the ability of a red light camera from being able to get a clear and recognizable image of your plate number.

Can't get a traffic ticket while riding a bicycle.

Truth of Fiction? **Fiction**.

It's true that you could be cited for things such as a red light or a stop sign because many of the vehicle code violations are applicable to bike riders. But the California DMV makes it clear that "Violation points are assigned to Vehicle Code sections...involving safe operation of a motor vehicle." and "Any violation occurring as a...bicyclist has no point assigned." Before you sign the ticket make sure the officer made some indication on the ticket that you were on a bike. If not, than if/when the DMV were to receive notice of the ticket they may assign points to your driving record, not knowing you actually got the ticket while riding a bike.

Automated camera enforcement is only used to issue red light tickets.

Truth or Fiction? **Fiction**.

The majority use of automated camera enforcement is for monitoring red light violations. However, tickets for improper turning movements or failing to stop for a railroad crossing can also be issued via automated methods.

Attending Traffic School will remove a ticket from my record.

Truth of Fiction? **Fiction**.

Traffic School can no longer be used to obtain dismissal for convictions. Traffic school completion will only allow for one conviction within an 18 month period to be held "confidential" so that both the court and DMV have the ability to view the conviction but it will be held confidential to insurance and other companies.

Traffic Tickets "fall off" a driving record after a couple of years.

Truth or Fiction? **Truth**.

Most traffic violations will remain on your California Department of Motor Vehicles driving record for a period of several years, but do eventually "fall off." Traffic violations that are assessed one point by the DMV (i.e. unsafe lane change, crossing double yellow lines) remain on your record for three years (counting from the date of the violation). More serious traffic offenses carrying more than one point (i.e. DUI, Speeding over 100 mph) remain on your record for about seven years from the date of the violation.

Autos with trailers are permitted in carpool lanes as long as passenger requirements are met.

Truth or Fiction? **Fiction**.

On most California highways those towing trailers have to drive at reduced speeds and sometimes are even restricted to stay in the far right 2 lanes. Therefore you cannot drive in the carpool lane if you are towing a trailer (big or small) regardless of whether you have the required number of passengers in your vehicle.

An officer cannot pull you over for just a seatbelt ticket because it is only considered a secondary enforcement law in California.

Truth or Fiction? **Fiction**.

There was once a time when a police officer could not pull you over only for a suspected seatbelt violation because it was only considered a secondary enforcement law in California. Around 1993 seatbelt violations became a primary enforcement law in California so now you can pulled over for just that, and seatbelt tickets can put points on your record depending on the type of seatbelt ticket you receive.

If the officer makes a mistake on the ticket, no matter how small, it invalidates the ticket.

Truth or Fiction? **Fiction**.

Most mistakes, such as incorrectly spelling your name, writing your address down wrong, or marking your car as silver instead of beige, can go to show the officer was not paying full attention to detail or was distracted, but it is extremely rare that such a mistake by itself could actually invalidate a ticket. That's not to say there are no "fatal mistakes" an officer can make. For example, if an officer tickets you for failing to stop for a Stop sign and writes down the incorrect location on the ticket. If you can prove that intersection doesn't have a stop sign, then the officer's mistake may very well lead to dismissal of your ticket.

I can tell the court my speedometer was off and get out of a speeding ticket.

Truth or Fiction? **Fiction**.

The fact of the matter is that you were still speeding. What you are arguing is that you didn't know you were speeding, so the fact that your speedometer was off does not result in an automatic win for you. A court may however be gracious if you have written proof that your speedometer was diagnosed and repaired, and the difference between your cited speed and the speed limit is less than or equal to the amount by which your speedometer was off.

Court Information

As you know by now, not every ticket is dismissed by using a Trial by Written Declaration. The beauty of a Trial by Written Declaration in California is that it actually gives you two bites at the apple. If your ticket is not dismissed, you are actually right back where you started from and can request an in-court trial just as you would have if you hadn't filed a Trial By Written Declaration at all. However, when going to court, you should be aware of how to present your case properly so as to maximize your chances of getting your traffic ticket dismissed. In this section we have put together all the information you will need to fight your traffic ticket in court. Before you read this information, please make sure you take note of our housekeeping disclaimer below.

Good Housekeeping Stuff: TicketBust.com is not a law firm. The following is intended by TicketBust.com to provide information related to traffic tickets in California that can help you prepare for your day in court. It is based on opinion only, is not legal advice, and is for informational purposes only. TicketBust.com consultants cannot advise you on what to say in court or offer you legal advice. If you need legal advice you should consult with a lawyer.

About the New Trial

If you were found guilty after submitting a Trial by Written Declaration to the court the next step most beneficial to you is requesting for a new trial; or a *trial de novo*.

Going to Court for the New Trial Is a Good Thing

The new trial provides you a second opportunity to have your ticket dismissed. Your original Trial by Written Declaration should not be taken into account - you can change any of the information you present in court, add any new facts you wish to, and you can bring witnesses to testify on your behalf or photographs, diagrams, etc., for the judge to consider.

The Majority of Cases Where the Officer Doesn't Show Up Are Dismissed

Generally the only witnesses at the trial are the officer and you, the defendant. If the officer fails to appear at trial the judge may dismiss the case entirely without any action by you. If, for whatever rare reason, the court were not to automatically dismiss your case, you could always simply ask the court to dismiss the case in the interest of justice based on the lack of prosecution (the officer not being present in court means there is no witness to disprove your innocence).

If you like to sound more technical, you could also refer the court to Penal Code Section 1385 (a) which says "The judge or magistrate may, either of his or her own motion or upon the application of the prosecuting attorney, and in furtherance of justice, order an action to be dismissed."

Be Prepared for Court

You should dress nicely (no shorts, tank tops, caps, sandals, or sun glasses) and show up to court at least 30 minutes prior to your scheduled trial time to ensure you make it to your court room on time. If you are not sure where to go, check in with a court clerk. Bring notes to help you remember how you plan to present your case to the court.

Relax, you are not alone

Many, many, people just like you appear in traffic court every day. The state even considers traffic infraction hearings to be "subordinate" judicial matters and permits trial courts to use temporary commissioners and temporary judges to hear traffic infraction cases.

Deciding Whether to Allow Your Case to Be Heard by a Temporary Judge

Temporary judges are usually unpaid volunteers, may not have as much practical experience in the legal issues commonly heard in traffic matters, and although they receive some training, they may lack the same experience and/or training that a full-time judge or commissioner has.

You Don't Have to Accept a Temporary Judge

If there is going to be a temporary judge deciding your case then you will be asked to "stipulate" (give your consent) to this and if not then you may have to come back on another day when a non-temporary judge is available. It is a matter of personal preference and you will have to make the decision yourself but some believe they have a better shot if they go before a "real judge" full-time judge or commissioner.

What to Expect in Court

First, the judge would generally welcome all parties to the courtroom and explain how the trial will proceed either verbally or through an information sheet handed out to you. You will be sworn in under oath to tell the truth and once your name/case is called you and the officer will be directed to go to your respective seats.

Next, the officer will be asked to state his/her name and then instructed to begin with his/her testimony.

The Officer Testifies First

When the officer finishes testifying you will be given the opportunity to question (cross examine) the officer.

Questioning the Officer

Questioning the officer can serve several purposes and you will want to refrain from becoming argumentative with the officer. Questioning the officer provides you the opportunity to clear up factual questions you have about the circumstances of the violation.

For example, if you are not sure how the officer was able to clock your speed while he was driving in the opposite direction, ask him to explain how your speed was clocked.

Ask Questions to Confirm Your Own Observations

For example, if you think you remember the weather was foggy and there was heavy traffic at the time you were cited you can ask the officer what the traffic and weather were like at the time to confirm.

Ask Questions to Set the Stage for Your Own Testimony

For example: If you ask the officer when his radar was calibrated and he tells you it was calibrated 3 ½ years prior to the date of the ticket you can make note of this and bring it up during your testimony that the radar was not calibrated within the last three years as required.

For example: If you ask the officer if there was notice of the speed limit in question (i.e. a visible speed limit sign posted) and whether he can testify beyond reasonable doubt that you passed by it and he says he cannot, you can make note of this and bring it up during your testimony (think: how could you be found guilty of doing, say, 35 mph in a 45 mph zone when the officer cannot testify that you passed a visible 45 mph sign in that area).

For example: If you ask the officer if there was notice of the Stop sign (or other type of sign it is alleged you failed to obey) and whether he can testify beyond reasonable doubt that it was visible when you passed by it and he says he cannot, you can make note of this and bring it up during your testimony (think: how could you be found guilty of violating the sign if the officer can't even testify that you actually passed a visible sign in that area).

Ask Any Other Questions You Have

You may find it helpful to stick to questions that require a "yes" or "no" answer or a brief, factual response rather than questions that give the officer a chance to state his opinion.

Ask questions that might uncover the fact that the officer was not in a position to see your vehicle clearly (if you can discount the officer's testimony you can show there is reasonable doubt that you are actually guilty).

When it's Your Turn to Testify

Asking the officer questions about his testimony or about other matters that related to your case, was not testifying. When it's your turn to testify, the judge will have explained you have a constitutional right to remain silent, but you give up that right when you testify.

If you testify you will have the opportunity to explain your version of what happened but this will subject you to being questioned/cross examined by the officer (or even the judge in some instances but the judge's questioning has to be fair or it is improper).

The benefit of the officer going first is you get to hear what type of case he has against you. You had the benefit of hearing him talk first and now have the opportunity to attack the weak or inconsistent parts of his testimony. Additionally if you received a copy of the officer's declaration before trial, which can usually be obtained by contacting the traffic division of the court, there may be a difference in what the officer says in court and what's written in his declaration. This will give you the opportunity to bring up any inconsistencies or inaccuracies that may discount the officer's testimony and be advantageous to you.

You can create doubt that officer's observations of your vehicle were accurate. If the officer made mistakes on the ticket this could also go to show he was not paying full attention to detail that day so that he may have misinterpreted the event leading up to the citation so you may find it helpful to work this into your testimony.

The Driving Conditions on the Day You Were Ticketed Can Work to Your Advantage

If there was heavy traffic around you at the time you were ticketed, or there was limited visibility, or the roadway was curved and hilly, these are all factors that can go to show the officer could not have had a clear view of your vehicle. (think: without a clear view how could the officer have accurately observed your vehicle to determine whether you committed the violation?).

If the officer is alleging you were issued the ticket because your driving was unsafe think of factors that would show your driving was not unsafe, for example there was no traffic, the weather was clear, there were no pedestrians anywhere around.

You should take notes with you to refer to, but avoid just reading the notes directly word for word, so you don't forget the points you want to bring up.

Tips for How to Present Your Case

When you are asked to speak you should be truthful; just remember that sometimes less is more! While whatever you say aloud should be truthful, you can leave out the parts of your story that make you look guilty. Speak in a clear, honest and convincing manner and avoid "iffy" type words i.e. like, possibly, maybe, if, or other similar words. Speak respectfully and control your emotions, and if you do not understand a question asked of you or a comment address the judge as "your honor" and politely ask the judge to explain to you.

Stick to the relevant facts of the case as you may only have a few minutes to present your case. Have your evidence in order (such as photographs, diagrams, medical records, car repair receipts, driver's license, auto insurance, or car registration documents) and have three copies of everything you bring with you in case the judge requests a copy for himself and the officer to view; that way you will still have a copy for yourself.

If you have any witnesses that you believe will support your case and you are ready to have them speak, ask the judge if it is the right time for you to bring up your witness; obviously, you should have prepared your witness ahead of time to make sure you agree on the same version of what happened.

Red Light Photo Tickets

Many people are intimidated to go to court for these types of tickets since they feel the evidence is right there in black in white (or rather color photograph). We feel it is worth having a separate section just for these types of tickets.

The officer may be a no show.

First, don't forget as we discussed before, the officer may not show up and your ticket might be dismissed automatically.

Even if the officer does show up, there are a lot of rules and regulations relating to red light camera enforcement and sometimes these tickets can be dismissed on a technicality if you find out a rule was not followed properly. One of these examples below may apply to your situation:

15 Day Rule

If you ARE the registered owner of the vehicle and the mailing date on the ticket is more than 15 days past the violation date listed on the top of the ticket, then you might try to get the judge to dismiss your ticket based on California Vehicle Code section 40518 (a) ("a written notice to appear based on an alleged violation of VC§21453 must be delivered to the registered owner within 15-days of the violation").

No Clear Photo of the Driver

If the photo of the driver is blurry or looks nothing like you, you might ask the judge for a dismissal based on lack of proof beyond a reasonable doubt that it was you driving the vehicle.

Mitigating Circumstances

Maybe you had a valid reason as to why it wasn't safe to stop when required, like a wet pavement, or another car was tailgating you, maybe you have a witness who will testify as to your reason for not being able to stop in time, or maybe you couldn't see the traffic light due to some obstruction like the sun, or a tall vehicle driving ahead of you.

Try to get the evidence the other side has against you such as the photographic evidence gathered by a red light camera thrown out!

The future state of red light cameras in California is questionable as more and more judges rule that the evidence gathered by a red light camera is inadmissible in court.

The California Court of Appeal in *People v. Borzakian* (2012) Second District Court of Appeal, Div. 7, B229748, reversed a decision to rule in favor of a motorist accused of failing to stop for a red light at the intersection of Beverley Drive and Wilshire Boulevard in the City of Beverly Hills in June of 2009. The camera generated photographs were taken by equipment maintained by a private camera company (Red Flex) and yet no employee from the camera company was involved with the trial, rather the case was presented by a Beverly Hills Police Officer.

The court ruled the officer's testimony failed to establish the photographs were trustworthy and that without proper testimony the photographs were not properly admitted, and without the photographs being admitted there was a lack of evidence to support the officer's claim that the motorist had run the red light.

The Borzakian ruling is also in keeping with an Orange County Superior Court Appellate Division case, *People v. Khaled* (2010) 186 Cal. App.4th Supp. 1, which similarly ruled that photographic evidence generated by an Automated Red Light Camera Enforcement System was inadmissible.

Citing past court decisions that have ruled evidence from red light camera tickets should be inadmissible may persuade your judge to throw out your ticket!

A Few (Quite a Few) Last Words About Court

Changing or Postponing the Court Date

If you need to change or postpone your court date you will need to contact the court as soon as you know you cannot make it. If the request is made when there is less than 14 days prior to your court date it is unlikely that the court will be able to honor your request.

If you fail to appear in court you may be penalized by a bail forfeiture (if you have previously posted bail with the court you will not be getting this money back), a conviction being placed on your driving record, a warrant for your arrest, or you may just be found guilty in your absence. The penalty will depend on the court, every judge is different.

Getting a Copy of the Traffic Survey or Similar Documents Relevant to Your Case Before the Trial

If you want to get your hands on something like a traffic survey for the street you were cited on to see if the speed limit is justified, most times a simple public records request to the Public Works Department in the city where you were cited or the City Hall will do the trick.

You could of course conduct your own discovery or subpoena documents from the police department where the officer who issued your ticket is employed for items relating to your traffic infraction case, for example: the officer's notes or the calibration records for the officer's radar, but this can be a time consuming process and it's also rarely done at the infraction level.

Furthermore, if you have a copy of the Officer's Declaration, which can usually be obtained by contacting or going into court,you may want to check this first as it may provide you with some of the same information you would have obtained had you sent a request to the police department such as the radar calibration record.

Asking to Have the Violation be Reduced

A reduction to a zero point or non-moving violation does not necessarily mean you will be getting any money refunded to from the court of the fine you paid for the ticket. It does however mean that no point would be going on your driving record and since there would be no point to affect your driving record, you would not need to pay the extra money or waste your time attending traffic school, so for many it is as good as a dismissal.

Speeding

If you are fighting a speeding ticket, you could respectfully ask to have the alleged violation lowered to a zero point violation, such as a coasting infraction 21710 (VC) ("Coasting in Neutral on Downgrade Prohibited") so it does not affect your driving privilege. Specify you are making this request with the intention that the reduced violation is to be in lieu of the court entering a finding of guilty as to the California Vehicle Code section for which you were originally cited.

Red Light

If you received a red light ticket, stop sign ticket, or other ticket involving a sign or signal, you could respectfully ask the court to lower it to a zero point violation, such as 38300 (VC) ("Unlawful to Disobey Specified Sign, Signal, or Traffic Control Device") so it does not affect your driving privilege. Specify that you are making this request with the intention that the reduced violation is to be in lieu of the court entering a finding of guilty as to the California Vehicle Code section for which you were originally cited.

Other

If this is NOT a speeding, red light ticket or a type of ticket involving a sign or signal, you could respectfully ask the court to amend the alleged violation to add a violation of the local

Municipal Code that is not a moving violation so it does not affect your driving privilege.

Specify you are making this request with the intention that the reduced violation is to be in lieu of the court entering a finding of guilty as to the California Vehicle Code section for which you were originally cited.

Requesting Traffic School

If you are requesting Traffic School, politely make the request and, since it can be beneficial, state a reason why it would benefit you. The trial judge has the power to order you to attend traffic school. If the trial judge believes that your circumstances indicate that you would benefit from attending traffic school, such attendance should be authorized.

If the judge denies you due to you having already been found guilty, be aware that according to Vehicle Code section 42005 (a) and pertaining to *People v. Enochs* (1976) 62 Cal.App.3d Supp. 42 and *People v. Wozniak* (1987) 197 Cal. App. 3d Supp. 43, you can still request to attend traffic school even after you have been found guilty of the alleged violation, if you were eligible for traffic school prior to being found guilty. The question of such imposition of traffic school should not be affected by the order in which plea, explanation and request for traffic school are presented as to decide on your entitlement to attend traffic school on the basis of the order of presentation rather than the facts of the case is capricious and arbitrary.

Receiving a Verdict

If the court has ruled against you (found you guilty) the decision is final. However you may be able to appeal it if you feel the judge made an error. You can contact the clerk of the court for the necessary appeal forms and instructions for filing an appeal if you feel an appeal is necessary; you generally have only 30 days to file an appeal.

If the court has ruled in your favor (found you not guilty or dismissed your case), congratulations! Get a copy of the decision notice so you have it for your records and if you previously posted bail (paid the fine for the ticket to the court) you will receive a refund from the court in the mail; usually within about 60 days.

Conclusion

So there you have it. The ones who "Got Off," and the ones who didn't. Hopefully by reading this book you can get off too.

Receiving a traffic ticket doesn't have to be a traumatic experience. You have options. Don't just roll over and accept the fine(s) and point(s) on your driving record. Do something about it as the people in our case studies have done.

Remember that all of the cases that we have presented here are based on 100% factual scenarios, although the names have been changed to protect the innocent. We tried to present these cases in a way that was factually true, easier to understand and provided just a bit of entertainment so it wouldn't put you to sleep. Hopefully we accomplished our objectives.

As this was the second book in our series *Traffic Tickets. Don't Get Mad. Get Them Dismissed.* I'm sure you can guess that there will be a third book coming down the line. Because you can't have a great trilogy without that third book. So, yes we do have plans for a third book. The details are still under wraps however, expect our third book to tie in many of the facts, resources, and concepts that we have brought forth in our first two books. Who knows, if that one goes well we may be forced to write a "Prequel" to our trilogy to let you know how this all began.

Until next time if you get a traffic ticket in the state of California, don't get mad. Get Them Dismissed!!!